WHITE SUMMER

WHITE SUMMER

Poems by John J. Herman

New York

Cover Design by Ronnie Ann Herman
Type Design by Ronnie Ann Herman

FOR RONNIE

Who in the midst of midnight's dislocations,
Execrations . . . high exaltations,
Who in the corridors of sleep,
Thigh pressed to thigh, spirit to spirit
Pressed forever—who but you forever?

CONTENTS

BOOK I
(1977 – 1995)

WHITE SUMMER

THE BODY OF SUMMER

AFTER THE TORNADO

BOOK II
(1996 – 2005)

MIDDLE PASSAGE

SIMPLE DAYS

BOOK III
(2006 – 2009)

PARTS OF THE WORLD

BOOK IV
(2010 – 2012)

ON THE TIP OF THE TONGUE

BOOK V
EARLY POEMS (1963 – 1976)

LEMON LIGHT

HOW WE LIVED

BOOK I

(1977 – 1995)

WHITE SUMMER

OUT OF DARKNESS

Lucretius was wrong—everything comes from Nothing,
Being from non-being like water from a summer pitcher.
Earth tips on its axis, buds prong like small erections.
In the new-smelling, sticky, Corot sunlight,
Existence swoons in the ecstasy of becoming.

Darkness burns behind the socket of the sun.
The black holes of the universe
Pull with a tow tougher than a star's éclat.
Through the frog-spawn, fish-egg nebulae,
The black blood of creation churns.

Being is forever pouring into becoming.
Some cocky, fugitive principle
Fathers existence. Form from form from form
From Nothing . . . All is wonder,
Sheerest sortilege.

Over and over the miracle's performed:
Supernumerary existence bursts like popcorn.
Out of darkness, light.
Out of the yawning, inevitable vortices,
The hoopla of becoming.

I STAGGER UNDER THE WEIGHT OF THE SUN

I stagger under the weight of the sun,
Life snares like grass at my ankles.
From the woods the cuckoo launches its reiterant cry.
An odor—part excrement, part vegetable exuberance—
Throbs like a migraine through the fields.

Already spring has stumbled into summer,
Trees whir like over-wound alarm clocks.
Under their weight the flowers ooze and bleed.
The morning rests on its haunches,
Cow-heavy with the juices of time.

See how the mountains soar in the air!
Who holds them on his back, his heart a puddle of sweat,
Dreaming of shadows in the coil of noon?
Who labors with the goldenrod?
Clouds pass, empty as the thoughts of God.

Where is the seed unhungered for the soil,
Where the untrammeled ghost?
Thorns tear at the passing thigh,
A fish bone waits for the throat,
Hair glistens like peach fuzz down the lovely spine.

A DAY IN THE COUNTRY

Summer like a pair of swollen nipples!
Leaves in the trees,
Berries popping in air,
Hornets bullet angry—look!
The incredible, recurrent miracle.

Summer smells of piss and lavender—
God's grand coronal
Falling like dirty linen.
Now your feet dig in the rusty needles.
Will you pant like a dog? Will you weep? In the heat
Your heart simmers like a cooking turnip.

April, raw as a skinned knee . . .
May, the unguent . . . August is a balloon
Escaped from a child's hand,
Up and up and up . . . .

Arms lips tears sweat sighs—
Summer keeps scribbling its potboiler epic.
Then evening, a haze of gray,
A puff of smoke in the cloudy brain.

                        Day dies,
Paris the pretty-boy draws back his bow.

STORY

Heat . . . and then more heat.
The day stokes up like bread in an oven.
Beneath the sky, sweaty as a janitor,
The waves roll in like beach balls.

Children are shouting in the surf.
By the pines a woman changes her bikini.
The winds go poking in the wind-drift—
Rubber, dried seaweed, baked tar. . . .

Along the dunes the sunlight peels the sand.
Gulls are soaring in the blue air.
In the distance, balanced like a nine pin,
A tanker teeters on the horizon.

This could happen any day,
Any Sunday pricked by salt and sand.
The ages piled for this—
Small change in your pocket.

Butterflies are fluttering by the Pillars of Hercules.
The ocean curves its palm.
Suddenly, poised on the edge of immensity,
The tanker drops like a stone into nothing.

DO YOU REMEMBER?

We pulled the row boat
across the postage stamp lake,
and in ten minutes—
blisters like burnt rolls!
You'd think we were adolescents,
outstripping the pimply lovers
to seize our thicket! . . . There,
under the Chinaberry bushes,
my fingers found you . . .
out of sight is out of mind.
Or was it thirst
that parched like salt
where the grasses
sang like water?
Who can explain
the sun like sizzling butter,
or my mania
for your sharp tits?

SUMMER HEAT

Even the wasps were stunned by the heat.
The wind brought no relief,
Puffing like a broken vacuum cleaner.
The overburdened air

Smudged the shadows like a thumb.
This was summer, the bull's eye,
The unimagined. The sun
Went in and out of focus like a telescope . . .

You yawned, you nodded,
You sweated in the heat of afternoon.
You slept—and the *Times*
Slipped like a letter to the floor.

The eye fills up with seeing . . .
All day I went round and round,
Writing poetry. Summer . . . summer!
Hornets hung like paint from the rafters.

You slept like ripened fruit,
Pregnant as pregnant, beached
By the cycle of life. Dust to dust,
Life from offered life. Outside,

Sunlight riveted the flowers.
Promptly at five, rain
Rattled the windows,
Fell like seed on the starving lawn.

VIRGILIAN SUMMER

Virgilian summer draws to a close.
Crickets in the tall grass
Churr in the gathering darkness.

Now the insects dance in the air,
All things quiet with the night,
Twilight thickens in the branches.

A bullfrog coughs at the water's edge,
A small bat weaves in the dark. From a barn
A farm dog barks in the lengthening silence.

HOME FROM THE COUNTRY

Under the window the locust
Cracks in the heat. Cars whiz on the avenue,

Dog shit piles in the park. Home from the country!
You wander from room to room,

Searching for—what? A book?
A forgotten letter? . . . This is your life,

Collected as in a telephone directory.
Hold it in the palm of your hand.

Light from off the farther buildings
Flares like arrows in the sun.

From across the park the sun
Nails your palm to the corner of the wall.

WHITE SUMMER

White summer, you held me in your arms,
And whatever I wanted, you gave.

There is a law that states
Even to glance backward is dangerous.
Orpheus learned this,
Lot's wife was turned to a pillar of salt.
So on summer nights with the sound of traffic,
With the sound of traffic underneath the window,
You feel the downward grip of gravity,
The subtle certainty of our passing.

There was a stream that held us,
The sunshine said be happy!
The road went running away over the hills
As if it were alive . . . Happiness deserves its history,
And continues on its way a little while,
Filled with details like a field with flowers.
We walked through meadows, and the summer sun
Fell on our shoulders like an avalanche.

Flies, starlings, a yellow salamander
Brilliant as citron. . . Hornets
Blundered in the rafters.
Two hundred miles away, the city
Simmered in sweat and confusion.
White summer, you held me in your arms,
And whatever I wanted you gave—
Heat, silence—the center of the diamond.

I THOUGHT IT WOULD NEVER END

I thought it would never end,
Those summer days
When I made love to you
On Park Avenue,
My heart ablaze in midsummer's blaze,
Crouched at the edge of the bed,
The animal absorbed to the preternatural.

Yes, we were hardly aware,
Sunk in the body,
And light as air,
Your body
A field of grasses where I played;
Invisible as reflex as we lay
In the first fierce blush of pleasure.

What we were then I cannot say,
In the intense rigidity of repose,
Caught in the grip of common serendipity
Where ghost cries out for hair and bone:
You you you you you
And I alone forever!

And so improvident we lay
And spent ourselves away,
Thinking it could never end.
Like beams within one light,
Or beads upon a string,
Pulled taut into the air,
And wetted in the wind until it sing.

SPLENDID DEATH

The leaves, the leaves, the beautiful leaves
Blow at their ease in the autumn breeze.
Lift up your head, said the red said the blue,
All up and down the avenue.

O splendid death with no place to go!
The trees are plugged in like Christmas trees.
O marvelous color, O bread and butter
And wine—spilt wine.

A carnival feast for a cannibal king,
These lollipops, these shiners
That stick in the eye, that stick in the eye,
Blue sky blue sky blue sky—and leaves!

Gold leaves mold leaves red leaves dead leaves,
Howling—and silent as blood.
O ancient tale! O stick-in-the-mud!
Poor death. Poor eternity.

AUTUMN EXPIRES

Now Autumn fêtes the eye,
Red and rust and russet
Burning like a martyr on a spit!
The mind feeds and feeds,
As if it had no friend but the weather.

Why does Nature need this excess?
The muscular satisfaction of distance
Abutted by the half-tone of the trees.
Who planned this auto-da-fé,
These leaves that get thrown away like candy wrappers,
This ruddy, corrugated surface,
This now?

Autumn expires,
Violence subsiding into smoke.
The sky hangs like a curtain at a theater.
The maple drops its light,
A leaf
Flutters in the crown of a tree,
And the wind
Rustles like a vacant hand,
Wind in a chimney,
Emptiness at the elemental center.

WE STAND TOGETHER IN THE CATTLE CAR

We stand together in the cattle car
Nose to nose and flank to flank—
Cigarettes in a dirty pack. Flesh is grass,
Stale tobacco and the stench of dirty clothes.
The subway in the tunnel rocks and reels
Like blond Achilles with an arrow through his heel.
Where are we going now? No one knows.

To offices, to classrooms—God knows where!
The daily flushing of the subway tube
Washed like Lazarus into the air.
Each carries his Anchises on his back.
The day that history ceased but no one cared
History kept going like a wind-up toy.
(It's not a story that the tongue gets right,
The words have lost their meaning, the teeth their bite.)

No one cared and no one even knew.
The rain is falling on my father's city
Like black blood from the severed prophet's bones.
Rivers drive about the island of Manhattan.
Where is the correlate to all this empty noise?
The glitter for those towers in the air?
We stand in the rain, waiting for the bus,
The past weighs down upon us like an incubus.

BLIZZARD

All day the snow comes smoking down,
By three the air is dark as ink, shiners
Puff about the eyes of the street lamps.
The cars stand stalled in ice, humped
Like buffalo at the corners. Streets are coated
As a tongue after three days of fever.
People lean into the wind, heat bleeds
Like smoke from factory chimneys.

Between the slap of the tires and the motors' growl
The heart hesitates. Nothing blooms from this center,
Only excitement like static electricity.
All pelts helter-skelter in this cyclotron.
In one gulp winter swallows the city.

MARCH IN CENTRAL PARK

A rising wind, the March birds twitter,
A gathering thunderhead
Darkens the horizon like thought.
Then the sun, a whiplash in the eye—
Spring goes off like a firecracker.

A wisp of blond, a strand of yellow—
Straw in the hair of a girl.
Only man won't resurrect, caught in his nose dive
Across the forehead of the day.

Young men are doing kung-fu in the park.
The women break out hats and gaudy dresses.
The children shout and call,
Chasing the trajectory of their falling ball.

THERE AND BACK AGAIN
HBH

Open your eyes and it is summer.

Open your eyes
and the trees are graced with green,
cloud hungry,
stretching their necks like young giraffes.

Close your eyes and it is winter,
the indigenous,
the slate gray monster with its gargoyle smile
working its erasures like white-out.

Who can explain this coming and going,
this trafficking?—
an antediluvian equation
in an outworn arithmetic.
All is wonder . . . all is boredom.

Open the door and you are there beside me,
standing beside me
today, yesterday, tomorrow . . .
impossible.

Life gets snuffed up,
ammonia in the nostrils of some god.

The cracked cup fills with water.
The bole of the flower
swings on the rinsing wind.

THIS MOMENT

This moment is the last.
And this! And this!
The flutter of all things green,
Leaves leaping, light breaking,
Buds bursting in
Peacock-tail exuberance,
Again! Again!

Dogs sniff the demotic hydrants.
A softball smacks the air . . .
A day like any other,
Without meaning or significance,
Under the trichrome trinity
Of leaf and sky and cloud.

A momentary conviction in a park;
A handkerchief expanse of sky;
An island of deciduous green
Transfixed by the universal vision.
This paradise! . . . fool's paradise . . .
This Now.

Adipose instant where we rest
On the grass, with insects
And the whiff of sewers;
Where the fat squat pigeon
Leaps into the air—and soars!
Touching the zenith.

THREE POEMS FOR R.

i

No matter how long the time's not long enough.
Although the horizon stretch to the hairbreadth line
Where earth abuts the evening's technicolor,
The sky vaults upward into blueblack darkness,
Into indelible ink. Too many things
Cry out to us for love. The earth
Curving beneath its mat of green;
Children's bones waxing to completion;
Winter twilight in the sticks of the trees.
It comes to this inevitable declension,
Quotidian miracles thicken the blood.
The lungs ache with the copperpenny ache
Of breath, in the exultation of losing.

ii

There always comes a time to say good-bye.
The floors are swept, the door is shut and locked,
The walls stand vacant as a face
After another face has gone. Farewell!
This is the moment you foresaw
When the car stood idling in sunlight,
And vagrant summer bounded up the stairs.
August, a bar of soap left on the ledge,
Gives up its scent. The road expires.
The dust of afternoon lies heavy in
The folded curtains. Graying bread crumbs

Stale in the pantry. A lazy long black snake
Suns at ease along the patio wall.

iii

Love, the drip-drip of this middle aged heart
Is sap from a tree, the indelible green drool
Of the bathroom's platinum faucet, or
The rattle of salt through the hardening veins.
How can it be that, winded, we have come
To where (with gray in our hair!) the valley
Deepens on either side, the ridge
A knife-edge between our teeth? Was it yesterday,
Or was it only yesterday, the blood
Blushed like pomegranate, fancy free,
In the dripping, boatsize bathtub? This drip
Is love, my love—the winding climb
To arrive back safely where we began.

WHAT I WANTED TO SAY

What I wanted to say
was too hard—like nails
driven into boards
that won't budge
and gouge the hands.

Everywhere a message,
a vibration,
the cheapness of flesh,
the redundancy of distance.

Your hand kept touching
the soft spot at the throat
woven like gold
in cheap upholstery.

I'm in love with the sun
that's lent for a day,
a cup of milk,
the happiness of children.

What I wanted to say
was hard—and hurt!
A message, an unmeaning . . .
the rush of blood
shot from the ruptured aorta.

THE BODY OF SUMMER

THE HEIGHT OF SUMMER

From the height of summer, the gazebo,
The pavilion with the roof of shiny tin,
Above the mountains, above the fields,
Every instant is the instant of our death.

Every hour is the hour of completion,
At the zenith, with the patina-ed leaves,
With clouds passing over in perfect progression
Above the orchard, above the orchard's crop.

And sometimes you can see behind the leaves
The darkness at the summer's center,
The pip where the berry's sap
Puddles in excess down the lily's throat.

And from the height of summer you can see
The axis turning slowly on its track,
The fallen meteor burning in the grass,
The circle closed, the fiery banner streaming.

You can see the leaves of fifty summers
Gathered on a single stalk, a flower,
And at the center, where the silence lies,
Darkness where the coiling serpent waits.

MY METROPOLITAN MUSE

My not impossible muse!
Do you remember that summer
When day after day
In the boilerplate heat of August
I wrote you poetry?

That inspiration hung
With the scent of garbage in the air!
The stench of cabbages,
Grease from a delicatessen,
Fumes from a standing taxi.

Yes, dragging between two blocks
In the slowmotion tidal heat,
It was always you I'd meet,
You in the traffic on the street,
The women on the steaming concrete
With the half moons of perspiration at their armpits.

My metropolitan muse!
The moon is a sack of nostalgia
Hung out like laundry between buildings.
Any street could lead me back to you,
My long-leggèd darling!
Every signpost was an arrow
Pointing to you!

GOLONDRIA

Swallow,
small spindle
swift needle
over the steeple
into the eye . . .

Nothing
should astound,
neither the traffic
moving
nor the traffic
standing still,
the slimness of
your waist, or
the small pinkness of
your tongue.

Swallow,
you will not return,
though spring
quicken the forsythia.
The new bird
with straw in its bill,
the old nest
with dirty paper.

NOTHING ADDS

Extravagant beauty of the leaves,
Gleam of spider, glide of gull,
Glint of hair on hair.

I keep on trying to express
What is wordless
And comes to nothing:

The apple on the bough,
The apple in the hand,
The apple in the throat:

Gold and gold and gold.
Your figure disappearing in the dark,
A swallow disappearing in the dark.

A WORD. A GRAIN OF SAND

Again... again... again!

A flash of steel. A glint of chrome.
The tinfoil whiplash of a windshield.
These things that undid you
To your profit...

The ululation of the wind,
The animadversion of the light
Spitting its incantations:
Wings that brush you in their flight.

Everything is done, undone
In the wink of an eye,
O, Adam in Paradise with untaught tongue!
The bite of things that surprise:

A word. A grain of sand.

TORSO

A violence of sunlight in the trees,
Thunder in the leaves,
The weight of the sun in the blood—
Again! Again! We are plunged
Into life.
Who could keep his fingers clean?

The trees at evening
Changing to shadows,
Or rooms
With the odor of evening,
The checkered light
Falling on walls,
The patterned light
Breaking on stones . . .

Importuned,
Like Apollo from the clouds,
And lose our soul
For a reed . . .

A thinking reed.

THIS BODY OF SUMMER

This body of summer glittering with heat,
This mica of the sea; platinum trail of insects
Where shadows stain and stems foretell
A legend of flowers. Softness remembered,

Almost forgotten, and musk of the ripened bole;
Weight of ribs in the sand
Where summer grips the nostrils,
And eyes are press in cartwheels.

Hills under the fingers exhibiting the sun
Once, and then again, and then forever
In the lengthening mythology of memory—
This body of summer unquenchable,

This miracle of rust and spores,
With dancing light above the waves,
And mountains breaking into light,
Where massive shoulders bear

The weight of the world, the earth's pressure.

BEGIN NOW

This stone that you lift, this weight of the sun,
And the small star at the corner of the sky—
Your destiny perhaps no more than this.

Begin now the unending song
That comes with light, that glitters with morning,
And never ceases to amaze;

Begin the arcane syllables of praise
In a city of closed spaces, in a nettled field,
A room with swinging shutters;

The esoteric vocables of salt
Hurtling through archways in hidden places,
The rush of water over twisted faces

In a space to which at last you come,
Sand in sandy bottoms where you pass,
Legs planted, feet planted in the sand,

The dragonfly alight amidst the grass.

SEASCAPE

Where the arc of the sea
cuts the curve of the sky
a wind was blowing.

The waves rolled in,
green and silvergray,
billowed in swells.

Winds licked the ocean,
muffed the extremities;
the deep umbrageous seaweed tongued.

A boat was crossing
where sea gulls beveled and veered,
white sails huffing in the blue.

O, ceaseless combination,
where sun combusts on wave,
and the shattered crown curls downward,

churning to darkness.

THIS BANQUET, THIS SCANDAL

These things you held in your arms,
Earth, a handful of petals, the sea,
A park hidden between buildings
Where you paused daily; flesh
(That fruit at your mouth) . . . these things
You knew a moment and loved
(Always astonished, always afraid!),
Your eye reached out to touch
This banquet, this scandal—
These things that bound you to the earth—
The apple and its bruise.

CRICKETS

You have come this far.
The path gives out beyond the lot,
Among the weeds, among the burnt up grasses.
Here you have come at the end of summer,
At the very end of summer,
With the sound of crickets.

You have been here before,
Others have been here before.

At least there is a glimpse of sky,
A wisp of cloud,
The odor of new turned earth.
If only there were someone at the other end
Where the path goes down to darkness,
Someone with whom to speak
In intimate brief colloquy . . .
But no. There is only
This glint of summer with its presage of autumn,
The solemn steady beat of being alive.

You have come this far.

Except of course for the crickets,
Which might have brought you here in any case—
A twittering in the grass, a crying in the air,
A booming in the steady summer fields.

SWALLOWS

Swallows in the evening air
Glitter and glide.
The leaves are edged in light,
Golden light
Trailing across the earth like hair.
The earth awaits beneath its crown of stone.

Day dies. The swallows
Wheel and dive in perfect formation,
Night comes on—a dark place in the throat,
And stars prick out—first one, then one,
Here and there and there,
Legions in impossible space.

You wait in memory at the edge of a field,
Non-mythological you,
A woman I have touched.
Now in the air with flowers,
With the scent of flowers,
You return like a stone to the hand,
A perfect stone in the palm of the hand.

The fields rise up to greet us,
Pull us down in their long embrace.
They say love rules the world,
And set it on its way through endless space,

And I believe them. Love,
A rush of wings. A quickened match.
A flame that finds you for an instant
And then goes out.

GOLDEYE

August opened and closed—
A gold eye in the forehead of the day.
The wind whipped its tail among the sassafras.
Whatever happened was quotidian—
A nail through the fleshpot of the hand.

I remember rocks where the sun rested.
A lizard blinked its eye. The landscape flamed—
Yellow, then orange with a streak of red—
Blackened like burnt paper.

The ring we gave betrothed us to the earth,
The sweatshirt of love incinerating to ashcan.
We lay in the heat like stranded whales,
Your arm arched me like willow.

Later there were only leaves in alleyways.
The shutters on the avenue slammed down.
A cloud passed—an eyeball at the bottom of a well.
The arteries sang and sang—a knife at their throat.

OPEN YOUR EYES

Open your eyes and you will see
The mountains leaping into light,
Pine needles trembling in sun,
Clouds speeding over the hills.

Only a thimble full of light
Will fill your eye like an eggcup,
Flooding the everlasting valley
With primal, unimpeachable gold.

THIS ALPHABET

This alphabet of half-finished things,
these a's and b's
of trees and leaves,
a flame, a finch's feather;
this immanence—gray eminence
where the word
was first written, first heard
in belch and bellow
of thunder
where eye first knew
the incommensurable.

This chemical soup, this stuff,
is alpha and omega—mere dust,
a puff of dust
upward to endless silence, where
a god resides, sleepless, without
the beat, the bloodheat of
the eagle's wing.

THE THROAT OF SUMMER
For my daughters

Into the chalice of summer
Swollen with light,
The mansion of green,
The garden where the hummingbird
Hovers, by the hedgerow,
By the darkened pool,
The diver, the dancer descends.

And you lean to touch the lips,
The smoothness of the brow,
Tracing the nostrils where
The child sleeps, her breath
Perfuming the air; seeing
The delicate shoulders
Beached like a keel; you walk
In sadness, in dolor, bending
To kiss the fingers, hearing
The grasses ringing,
The mermaids singing,
The tintinnabulation of the fields.

Into the bead of light
The diver, the dancer,
Where the lily
Moves in whiteness,
In stillness, beside
The flower,

The throat is laid
Beneath the knife
Forever.

OUT OF THE FOUNTAINHEAD

Out of the fountainhead,
The summer's pod,
The golden throat
Spilling with light,
In the midst of life
Green genesis!
The serpent in the ear
Hissing,
That sac of fecundity,
That stalk, that tower

That tinderbox!
Out of the thunderhead
The tale told over again
Of bud and bush and flower
And honeyed gland
And Adam born of the earth,
The root in the heart
Swollen with blood,
The tip of light,
The beam, the shaft—
The shaft in the heart.

HARVEST

This legend of summer,
This grit of the sun,
With rocks breaking into waves
Wherever you look,

And sunlight on the grass
(O daughters with sandals!)
And plotless paths of light
Between the grass!

What harvests! What granaries!
The shell of the ear
Pressed to the earth,
The calyx of stone.

Such voyages, such distant headlands
Like shattered colossi,
The crust broken, the earth broken,
The finger the eyelid the eye,

The mouth bloody in the noonday heat
With the weight of the sun
Chock-a-block on your shoulders,
With fields with snakes and children,

The heavy horses stomping for the barn.

AFTER THE TORNADO

THE EPIC

For —

Who said there had to be a voyage? . . .

Actually,
There was only a single day, with laughter,
With colors like a child's bandana.
You lay on your back in the sun
And sunlight polished the table.

At ten
Marriage bells shattered the silence.
The bridegroom sent you home,
Your breasts too young for the marriage bed.
You laid the memory away,
Spice and linen for a dowry.

At noon you suckled your man
With the hot milk of the sun,
You laughed when it spurted like water—
Forgetting your father, forgetting your mother
In the first fierce blush of pleasure.

Groin is pressed to groin
Where the sun burns skin from the shoulders.
The tremor of the earth, the shudder
Of a man and woman.

You crouch in childbirth
In pain and disbelief: sweat,

Mucus, blood . . . a cry
That will echo for a lifetime . . . For this
You came into the world!

The wrinkles of afternoon thicken.
Those thighs, that once-loved man—
You are almost indifferent.
You recall the morning of your youth
When life was sharp and pungent as fenugreek.

At five you sip your tea,
Intelligence the best companion.
There is gray now in your hair.
What have you accomplished?
Painted a picture? Raised a child? Built a barn?
Praise lies all about you, if only you'd look,
Like sun on the face of buildings.

Night comes, and the odor of paludes.
Your single day is drawing to a close.
In dreams you don your hennaed garter
And go to meet the legendary bridegroom . . . .

This epic was only an instant, this novel
A single page.

THE PROMISE

I am sending this letter to remind you
you promised to love me forever. I was writing
an epic, it was almost completed
when you left. I didn't abandon poetry,
poetry abandoned me . . . Sometimes
I lie awake, imagining
you will never return. You must remember
those churches we visited together,
the Gothic cathedrals, and the small one
whose name I forget,
in the block around the corner.
I wouldn't want to live without such structures,
buildings to capture the sacred
as water in the palm of your hand.
Since you've gone the nights are quiet,
the covers no longer kicked to the floor.
Often I meet myself coming or going
or miss myself entirely on the stairs.
You'd hardly recognize me. I wonder,
would I recognize you? The bed is cold,
the desk empty. I miss you.

AFTER THE TORNADO

After the tornado we went swimming
at St. Mary's. There I saw a snake
the size of my arm, or your arm, actually,
humongous (as the children say),
swimming away with a whiplash
into darkness. The weather is hot,
we've written for a pool for the girls,
one of those plastic things, I suppose.
I'm still thinking about my dream, the one
where we stood in the garden.
Paradise must be that color. The sky astounds me,
such distance without meaning! Nightly
the stars prick out, the Rider, the Small Dipper, the Bear,
and the woman hung upside down in her rocker,
who is me, though I tell no one.
I suppose our parting was "for the best",
it was my idea as much as yours. Life's awfully short.
Thank Karen for the recipe. Do you remember
that Christmas long ago,
when I baked pumpkin bread for all our friends? . . .

JULY

For Henry Wells

i

Fat fat fat—
The white gull sheds its feather.

ii

The ocean is repeated and repeated
Until it has no meaning.

iii

The flowers outside the window
Are squawks of multicolored birds.

iv

Behold!
A piece of broken Mexican pottery.

v

The eye forages and forages
Under the dress of summer.

vi

A man knows and knows—
But only to the end of his nose.

vii

The world goes spinning
On its tippy toes.

MORNING TRIPTYCH

Have you seen that glitter of the sea
Winking, my man, winking from the window?—
There where the headland falls to a glassy surf
Sinister as compound inflation.
And the grass bends under the scythe of the wind
With a winnowing sound, the sigh of sleep
When you turn at morning on your bed,
And the dead brush lightly at the back of the eyelid,
And the mirror stands vacant, and the door to the closet
Opens on a passage as dark as an esophagus. Yes,
This whispering in the air would be quite lost
To dumbfounded ears, save for that sheen
Of polished mischief, that multiplied gleam
And sinister run and wrinkle of the sea.

ii

Contempt for my fellow man has coarsened my soul.
You are a doughpasted man, my wastrel,
My tadpole swimming in puddles.
Because of the milquetoast nature of reality,
You have contrived a theater in your skull,
My cineaste, my shooter of troubled propaganda.
A movie flickers at the back of your cranium.
Where is the hero of fourposted resolution
Who creates around him an aura
Generous as the enthusiasm for rock 'n roll?
Where the singer of unsouped superiority?
You've grown thin, my pudgy, grown waste,
In the vacant recess of a closet,

While your countrymen find the road to El Dorado
And wind it into a wetted, wadded ball.

iii

Here you breathe so much that is really you,
So different from those rooms with pasty faces.
Have you forgotten that engraved invitation,
The morning sun, a corridor of light against the wall?
Here there is so much that belongs to you,
A nexus of word and action as easy as inheritance,
An aboriginal instinct, an inspiration.
Sea sounds clash with the sounds of morning traffic.
Be thankful. Breathe deeply. It is time to get up.

PERFECT CENTER

To what purpose does August return
with blunt odors, bright days
submerged in pollen and sun?

The clouds pass over on the hills
where the distant cows
graze like children's toys;

but our days
shoot like arrows—
the bloodshot streak of the eye.

Sixty summers and it's over,
the compass of the hand
reaching forward, reaching back,

where you stand
in perfect center
in the fields.

SONG

Wherever the eyesight fall,
Kettle, basket, leaf,
There the tongue must speak
Its instantaneous praise.

Red berries on a bush,
A crack in the wooden floor,
Pine needles trembling in light,
Flames in the iron stove.

Soon the mouth begins
Its immemorial song—
A branch in the silent forest
Breaking the silence.

IN THE BEGINNING GOD CREATED NOTHING

In the beginning God created Nothing,
And Nothing moved upon the face of the waters,
And the black pines shook at the edge of the page.
Sometimes I suspect that faith must be
A letting go, a relinquishing;
For when we fall, we must fall
Forward, into Nothing. But if we lose ourselves,

Perhaps we are saved, like birds
That hurtle downward through air.
Behind the scrim of things, the screen,
The dance and dervish of deceitful sight,
The atoms are the merest fractures of the eye,
Tears in the projection of becoming—
And the name of this Nothing is God.

FOR MY DAUGHTERS

See how the brilliant flowers dance in the sun,
Filling this space, our earth, with gaiety;
See how they leap in light, spinning in light,
Like notes that spin within a symphony.

Thus everything completes its natural self
In miracle, seeing that nature is
Itself a miracle—at least today,
When Being lends itself this passing bliss,

Or almost so. I wouldn't overstate
The case, my precious ones, nor ever hide
From ready eyes the carnal mystery,
Teeth in the neck, claws sunk in the hide,

Love murdered on the mistletoe.
Yet everything turns bonny in the day
By fearlessly into itself ascending;
Yes, everything must give itself away

To find itself, back to itself descending;
Soaring away back to itself to come,
Like moisture in sap, sap in the flowers,
And flowers in the brilliance of the sun.

POEM

One poem can light a thousand days—
  As in an afternoon
  A thousand branches glitter.

One woman is all women,
  The fruit of Paradise—
  And always was.

One poem becomes all poetry,
  The word at the center,
  The green leaf on the bough.

FOR PETER

Though mocked by us when we were wise and young,
Arnold was right when all is said and done:
God is fled, this is the age of Iron,
Poetry alone can sing us back to Zion.

TIME IS JUST A WAY TO SAY GOODBYE

Places we have been before
Paddock hillock briar
By the dark entangled floor,
Time is just a way to say goodbye.

Poet tangled in a net
Noose nosegay knot,
Because of what is not,
Time is just a way to say goodbye.

In the labyrinth of cities
Traffic throbbing by the door,
Stop! the music blaring.
Time is just a way to say goodbye.

Time is just a way to say goodbye
To trapeze artist swirling
Above the net, the sawdust floor,
The hooded figure standing by the door.

By the rushing waterfall
Listen to the call of voices
Calling to the caterwaul,
Time is just a way to say goodbye.

Though you shout for more and more,
Though you eat the sun,
Because of what is said and done,
Time is just a way to say goodbye.

PHILOSOPHY

Plato thought it started in wonder,
The quickened flame at the center of the eye,

The heartbeat where the world arises
Heavy with light, shaking with light,

The jack-in-the-box appearance of the Now.
For me it starts in confusion.

Who can see the center of the wind,
Where God sits in manic isolation?

Who can touch the center of the night?
Darkness was before the light,

The shifting center of the self
Moving where I move,

The silent circle in the cricket field.
Light beats to blackness on the pines,

Stained to indelible darkness.
The thwart winds rattle the window frame.

I am alone
In the central loneliness of

Myself, this universe, this God,
In whose image I am.

TAKE WATER IN YOUR HAND

By a dark stream
Bend to the pure pollution,
Take water in the palm of your hand.

Take failure in your hand.
Bring to your parched lips
The bitter liquor of equivocation.

Accept at its elemental source
The waters of the chthonic,
The human, the mortal.

ZERO

This is zero. This the wall
Where you stand because you must—
The line you tow
Because you can tow no other.

And the spirit
Groans in the ache of its error,
Poison in its marrow,
A sliver, a dissolvent.

These lines are zero,
Crow's feet at the corners of the eyes,
Scribbles at the bottom of the page,
Stretch marks on the middle aged thigh.

STITCH

One time we walked together on this path
Through sunlight bland enough, I should have thought,
Along a lane that now, with autumn weather,
Tastes suddenly of those remembered days.
Autumn changes color and runs away.

And now, when all that's left is merely smoke,
I call to mind the generosity of flesh,
This transience that we shared a thousand ways,
Like an apple shared that made us happy.

And just last night when I was falling down
Into the valley of deep sleep,
I saw my father, restored to my own age,
His arms a marvel of muscled power.

Yes, here and here we passed, and I recall
A dress, a brooch, a strand of loosened hair,
Your lovely throat rippling in laughter.
A stitch a stitch a stitch and we are stitched
Like buttons to the bodice of the world.

PSALM

We are here, Lord, for an instant,
And when we go,
There is no returning.
You see the summer flies,
Sparks rising in darkness,
Petals of the myriad blossoming tree.

What can be our use, Lord,
What our calling?
For they are just who say
You remain,
We are thrown away,
You the overarching,
We the passing through.

God towers
Like cliffs out of the sea.
Height calls to height,
Depth to depth,
There is no surcease.
Tongue must tally tongue,
Eye the eye . . .

Here am I, Lord, here am I.

SEPTEMBER

A plate polishes to platinum, a pane
Flashes on nothing, and so
The year turns round, a blankness,
The weeping of the once green willow.

After the mugginess of August,
The rat-tat of distant thunder.
You wonder what god is dying in the forest
Where his fingers are broken like branches.

In the cottage the children are playing.
The clouds are dishrags in dirty water.
Gray now silvers your hair.
Your dress brushes the edges of the year.

The suitcase is packed, the briefcase,
The manuscript is stacked in the cupboard.
Papers are blown from the table, they disappear
Like bread crumbs in the gingerbread forest.

Somewhere in the forest a god is dying.
The goldenrod trails its fleecy poison.
From far away, with the insistence of a hammer,
Dull thunder rattles the window pane.

BOOK II

(1996 – 2005)

MIDDLE PASSAGE

BEGIN

Collect, and recollect,
And you are here, and it is now,
The ever immoveable present,
The opportunity. This is you,
This ceaseless progression toward a point
That is never achieved, belief
In whose existence is itself
An act of faith, an assertion against
The endless removals.
You are speaking in a voice
That is your own, a ceaseless meditation
In a dimension that is your loneliness.
Not the asseverations of youth,
Nor the wry evasions of middle age,
Nor the ancient aerie of age from which to view
Night and the cold fixtures of night.
This is you, speaking in a passion of improvisation,
A transcendence of the tongue
That cost you a lifetime—which was
Your life. The door is shut.
The paper is on the table.
It is time to begin.

REDUX

You start again at the foot of the stairs.
And when you pause at the top of the hill,
All is familiar. The landscape below
Lies quilted in autumn. You witness once more
The darksome continent stretching before you,
An inrush of being you thought inexhaustible.
You begin again at the start of the road,
A hint of deja vu in the dazzle of beauty,
Your instep fatigued, and the autumn wind
Bitter as aloes at the back of the tongue.
You see the highway stretching before you,
White light like dust stinging the retina—
And this, it seems, your only destination.

A MYTH

The house has stood for a year,
True juncture of light and oak
In the polished roofbeam. Where it stands
There was sumac, buckthorn, willow—
A pastoral. . . a wilderness.

The house has stood for a year,
Fledgling to a marriage
Of twenty; presence
That comes and goes with the weather,
Dive of swallow, flutter of leaf,
Flurry of falling snow.

                        You pray for something
To stop this disappearance,
(Delicate craft of shoulder, ankle, thigh);
Word or image or incantation,
Amulet or invocation—
Something beyond these things
That cannot stay. Spring.
A child. A kiss.

The house will stand for a year,
A decade. And where it stood,
There shall be talus. Burnt grass.
These things were permanent because
You were. A plight of the eye.
A pledge. A myth.

YOUR MILES WERE MY HAPPINESS

Your miles were my happiness.
Hills and headlong river,
Wold of tricky undergrowth,
Slap of sun on stone,
Flush of alluvial plain—
Stretch now under this light.

But there we also spied
Foxes in the fields,
Moles maneuvering for crevices,
Noisome brooks
By darksome swale,
And lackluster tundra.

The clouds were dreams
In steady undertow
Where you lay you down.
Stubbed on being,
And caught between blades of grass—
No one has defined this happiness!

AND THIS YOUR LIFE

A tangle of loosestrife,
Willow, mallow, sage,
Moths mimicking sunlight,
Explosion of fireflies,
The distant explosion
Of Crab, Scorpion, Bear . . .

And here you lie—
A party to deer and hunters,
To adolescents humping in grass . . .
Creak of bough, sough of wind,
Susurration of busy insect—
And this your life!

May fire evade you.
May rain replenish your tables.
May suburbs avoid you where you lie,
Praying for a little luck,
A bit of patience,
Four corners pinned by a wall.

NO GIFT OF THE MUSE

Summer and winter and summer—
a cycle of blood,
a circuit of memory,
and we let go,
our little abnegations,
our small betrayals, only
the circle continues,
the landscape
stretching beneath you
like frozen music,
a deep vibration
stronger than the stomp of feet,
syncopation to some rhythm
almost forgotten,
winter and summer
in the public garden
with the odor of gardenia
among the years that are too much years,
a taste at the back of the mouth
like fever—but wait!
all is passing,
you cannot stave it, save
where the heart hesitates,
as when, pale as skin,
the moon
floats mid-sky
at noon of day.

STRAW

It was a dove it was a wave it was a candle.
It was blond light trilling against a wall.
It was music at the point of revelation
When words transform to images
And the world is a body of meaning—
This lily, this handful of straw.

GRACE

Now through the small house
Soft air is dancing,
So unlikely,
You might call it a miracle.

Absence is dancing,
You can almost touch it,
It brushes your skin,
It graces your eyes.

MIRACLE

Where the taproot sucks
Earth is broken,
Lips reach to touch
The moisture, the cleavage.

What is central remains—
Milk on a table,
Blood from your finger,
Beyond any syllable.

These things happened,
You entered in half-light,
Your clothing fell to the floor,
It was a miracle.

I held you in my arms,
You lay in summer's mantle,
The ocean closed above us,
I heard the suck of the sea.

Now in the gathering silence
I still remember
A single sentence—
The sigh of the curtain.

A STORY

Because it hung so simply on the bough,
you could not believe it would hurt you.
And so you enter the corridors of light,
but you are blind, you cannot see
the angels trafficking.
You pluck the fruit, you eat,
it is a familiar story; you cannot conceive
a meaning beyond this sussuration,
breath and the heat of breath
(though what is simple
can be mortal, the fatal banister,
the stairwell in the dark . . .)
Because it hung so simply,
you plucked—and tasted
a nectar you could never disown,
flesh and the flavor of flesh,
a place that is your own,
a death, a story.

MIDDLE PASSAGE

1.

When the flood came whelming in,
That would compensate for sin,
But this daily inundation,
Sunlight's morning celebration,
Rouses with a recognition
Of old Adam's manumission,
While the world is washed anew
In leafy green, in airy blue.

2.

God withdrew but to create
A world in which to pullulate,
Thus the space that He construed
Is where we all get f--ed and scr--ed.

3.

He was named an exegete
Of the modern Paraclete,
To celebrate on tin trombone
The advent of the ice cream cone.

4.

Before he leapt, the man had time to think,
This is the size to which the world must shrink.
Standing on his head, the boy could see
The vortex of the sky—infinity!

5.

These are the years that grave upon the face
Whatever is the opposite of grace,
And hang along the lineaments of sense
The rags and tatters of experience.

NEL MEZZO

Nel messo, or almost so—or more than so,
given our record. I always jumped the gun.
The first half I thought I'd lived before. Now
I peer into the depths but can't detect the bottom.
Life gets stranger, its prestidigitations,
its seedy, questionable legerdemain;
the old roué with a three-day's stubble
waltzes off with the beauty, whose finger
the rest of us couldn't touch . . . The flesh is sad,
and I've read most of the encyclopedias.
Moral complexity may be a credit to the dialectic imagination,
but it's the simple things on which I stub my toe.
Though waters run as deep as Hudson Bay,
when I dive, I suspect I'll crack my skull.

ON THE ROAD TO CECINA

On the road to Cecina we stopped to buy our daughter
Some white Italian shoes.
                         Have you seen those stones
That flash like silver paper in the sun?
These we saw in Elbe, where the waters rode
In aquamarine patches. There we peered
Downward to darkness where a green squid swam.
There the Italian girls went breasting the surf,
Topless as mermaids in the merry waves.
And there the lunar pebbles flashed like lightning,
Flashed like silver paper in the sun—
Just like the Italian shoes we bought our daughter!

AT EVERY CROSSROAD THERE STANDS A CHILD

At every crossroad there stands a child
Shivering, waiting to be born,
By every stream there lies a father
Cold in the water, dead as stone.

A breeze caresses the soft cheek's contour,
A green worm devours the rose,
An old house sags beside a river,
A girl deserts a town.

August kisses the golden woman,
Her breasts lick up the sun,
Autumn will crease her classic features,
Winter tear her hair.

Streams run, time flows forward,
Winter howls like a dog,
The locks are rusted, the windows broken,
The long tale never told.

A child cries at every crossroad,
Silence swallows his cry,
His hands reach out to touch the mother,
The winds whip at his eyes.

THE FALL

In August, at the edge of a leaf, blood.
And you foresee the passion that is to come,
Insect locked to insect in sexual ecstasy,
The entire contraption shuddering like an airplane shuddering,
Butting against the limits of becoming.

Praise the earth, light beneath a door,
Bones at the edge of a field.
The dead we have always.
Praise the beauty that is always present,
Like the breasts of a woman.
Praise the Lord, who was so obliging,
He consented not to be.

I sat in a garden, I walked by a shore,
I passed a field with new mown hay
Laid out in rows like the braids of a child sleeping,
Her arms thrown back,
Her forehead perspiring,
Her bones no stronger than a shell.
It was fear, Lord, it was trembling,
This passion under the fingers
That from a distance means nothing at all.

There is a voice speaking high in the air,
Like radio waves, maybe,
The way a man's beard keeps growing after he is dead.
There is a voice speaking, always,

If only you will listen.
And you stepped out onto nothing,
Gaily, like a child,
Your feet on nothing,
Like a soldier, as if you didn't notice,
You had such faith, I saw you floating,
The air as clear as water,
It flashed for a moment like water, and
You were floating—I saw you floating,

And then of course the fall.

YOU LET IT GO

You let it go, you let it go
small fish into water
round the corner, out of sight.
And the world was drowned in light,
dark spots before your eyes
where the bruises
smudge to blackness.

There is no holding
what is forever leaving,
no keeping
what is already departing,
the sound of a voice,
the grace of a word,
the shape of a hand;
there is only the repeating
of what you know already,
substance into distance,
distance into silence,
silence
into farewell.

You let it go, you let it go
flash of scales
round the corner
out of sight
where the mermaid
dolphinned into darkness
into lightness
into goodbye.

SUBLIME

This is the world in which we are lost.

And the valleys are throats that swallow,
The mountains sentences that astound.
We saw across fields, beyond meadows,
To a place we could never attain.
I touched every part of your body,
You touched every part of my body,
In a hunger that advanced us nowhere,
A passion for possession, a failure.

                              Darling,
What is the space for this love?
Is it the lungs gasping for oxygen?
Or the leaves flashing their silver?
Or is it the violence of the bullseye?
It was Adam, I suppose, it was Eve,
A garden from which to fall,
Chaos before the word—
Inarticulate imposition of the sublime.

THE DEAD

There where the weight of water
Breaks on the line of sand,
A mist drifts upward into the air
Wafted on winds that dog, that dog
The sharp-edged grasses of the shore.

And the paths lead backward over the dunes
Like so many sentences, air on air
Leading nowhere;
And the salt nets crack and dry
Where the dinghies loom,
And the undulant vast waters
Stretch to the flattened sky,
Pierced only by the cry and wheel of the gull.

And the rocks are beaten
By the ceaseless weight
Bearing down
To explode in dull thunder over
The ragged cliffs
Seamed as ancient faces;
Lengths of seaweed tangled as hair,
Broken teeth at the edge of the land
Where the adamantine ledge is pounded to pebble,
Beaten to sand.

I think of the dead,
Blown like mist on the air,
Crying with piteous voices,

And ravening for blood. Someday
Our voices too shall join that endless throng,
Querulous, shrill as birds,
Weightless as mist from the sea,
Without substance, without pain—
Except the ceaseless longing for what can never be,
The taste of salt and weight of the sun
And suck and sough of the sea.

PSALM

Lord, I confess my need
Indefeasible.
For everywhere I see
Brokenness. Eye knows,
Mouth tastes, hand feels
Foreignness, as when
A ball strikes, and sight
Reels in sparks.

We are in want, Sir,
We are in jeopardy.
We are hurled like iron hissing.
We are ice in a heated room.
We are broken shins.

This our state,
This our commonweal.
You are health, you
A rock in a slimy place.
Your face is hidden, your hand,
But here I stand,
I can do no other.

I need you.

SO BE IT

(After Montale)

. . . well, so be it. The mountain beetles in a tide-pool,
Sunset flashes from the horsefly's wing,
The sea comes home in pockets—dirty sand,
A shell, a strand of weed . . . Life, which seemed so grand,
Shrinks to no larger than your handkerchief.

SIMPLE DAYS

GOD'S WORLD

Wasps float through light,
Day fills the trees,
Leaves pattern the earth,

Sun illumined.
It is God's world,
My mother used to say,

Arching out of darkness
Like an eyeball. Breathe
The infinitesimal reticulations

Of being. Take in
Tree and tree and tree.
Now the shadows striate

The uneven sward,
Thickened to illimitable green.
The scythe of the sun

Descends
Upon the passing instant,
The waiting neck.

PERFECT DAY

No day so perfect as today!
Wind in the trees, clouds
Scudding the sky, light
Powdering like sugar—
It might almost be Paradise!

A black bird pecks in a furrow,
A window winks in the sun,
A scarecrow hangs from a stick . . .
The mind is at ease,
And everything is written.

JOHNNY CROW'S GARDEN
GBH

Holes are where things go,
Not what things are for,
The path can stretch from any door
To Johnny Crow's garden.

Down the familiar lane
Past the old turnstile,
Infinity, the sky
Beckons the wanderer.

This would happen when
Wandering as a boy
Life was counted on
Fingers and small toes.

But the old year goes
Drifting, and the new
Piles against the old
Outside in the cold.

Ah, but the roses too!

EVENSONG

In a troublous time
We think of cloves
A freshet of wings
The flesh of summer

Give us this day
Pines in the eye
Bread on a table
A happy child

Uncover a center
Beyond failure
Unshakeable music
A turret of words

AS YOU PASS

As you pass the public garden, you say
This is summer, the longed for,
The engine throbbing in the grass.

This the moment you wished for
With colors going in and out,
With shadows on the sides of the hills—

The season you foresaw
When branches were hard as iron
And earth as cold as stone.

Now green bugs sing in the leaves!
So you say, hold this, this water in your hand,
This passing, this irrevocable X!

GOLDFINCHES

Do you remember
the goldfinches in the pocket of sun
stitching the light?

And what we are
I can only guess,
based upon suppositions

that are themselves
hostage
to time and memory.

Nothing remains—
an afternoon
in shining light

where—now and forever!—
finches flecked in gold
flitter and fly.

THE BOOK OF METAMORPHOSIS

The Book of Metamorphosis has never been written.
It is your daughter who changes to a laurel
And flees within a stream. This is your life,
This transformation like sugar in autumn leaves.
And the mistakes you committed are entrances
Which bear your name, mirrors with familiar faces,
Pictures with features that are your own.

The Book of Metamorphosis cannot be comprehended.
It is a riddle at the crossroads—beast with the breasts of a woman.
The hand you held, the happiness, happened to someone else
In a different story . . . Now the field is ringed with flame!
A knight goes thundering through the wood; Alice
Falls through a hole. Small rain pierces the heart.

FAREWELL AND FAREWELL

i

Farewell and farewell and farewell!
So the insects kept singing
In August, in golden summer.

ii

It was a mother who read you a story,
Bending above you,
Repeating her words.

iii

It was a woman who said she loved you,
Straightening her blouse,
Smoothing her hair.

iv

It was a boat that sailed away,
Leaving water and emptiness,
Water and empty sound.

v

It was the cicadas in the trees
Singing and singing
In evening exultation,

vi

As when you were a child,
In the chorus of final summer,
Farewell and farewell and farewell!

SIMPLE DAYS

i

Simple days, and time is such,
You get little accomplished.
You walk to the end of the block,
See sunlight splayed on cars.
And the links form a bracelet
That fits your wrist, and the hours
Rise like pastry . . . Pigeons,
Bread crumbs, dried thyme . . . .

ii

Wind troubles the curtains,
A discontinuous music
Orchestrates silence. Few persons
Figure in this landscape,
An old man with a newspaper,
A young boy with a dog . . .
Let us praise grapefruit on a table,
A curtain, a silver spoon.
The ghost in the eye
Takes the pulse of winter,
And knows what it knows.

THIS IS WINTER

The trees are sticks. Great mouthfuls of air
Gape in the branches. The sky
Glitters through the abbreviations like teeth.
This is winter. It is pleasant to be inside
With snow licking the window,
With icicles and the flicker of snow.
Somewhere women still wear bikinis, children
Build sand castles, waves lap the shore. But here
There is no escaping the northward slippage, the drift:
The branch with the frozen paper in its crown.

"A CANDLE BURNS"
–Pasternak

The Christmas tree is brought again
And chained in its golden fire.
The children hang out trinkets on the boughs.
        A candle burns.

The snow is shaken from the eaves
Like powdered sugar. Winter nights
Caterwaul outside the panes.
        A candle burns.

The year turns round, its passing hours
Clasp hands together as we dance and sing.
The children put out milk in shiny cups.
        A candle burns,

And all grows silent. Now is the witching hour
When day is joined to day, year to year.
All is certain—all is passing here.
        A candle burns

And lights a corridor of other faces,
Other Christmases in other places,
Diminishing behind us like a wake.
        The candle burns.

*   *   *   *

Time is too short. We need Eternity
To stand among us like a Christmas tree.
We need the voices of the lovely dead
Choiring around us for their wine and bread.

We need the flowering in this little space
Of other measure and of other place,
Bound as we are in chains of hours and days,
To link us in a sacrament of praise.

*   *   *   *

The tree is hauled away. Its shiny balls,
Wrapped in paper for another year,
Lie close in cardboard boxes on the shelf.

The pantry's cleaned. Another term begins.
A few dried needles, rusted dirty brown,
Bristle in corners underneath the couch.

Outside the window, on the city streets,
The trees are toted up like logarithms.
Their arms flash tinsel in the gelid air.

L'HISTOIRE UNIVERSELLE

1.

Cain struck Abel with a rake.
All the blood of Eden could not slake
That angry wound. Eden fell
To stuff the hungry appetite of Hell.
Moses cleft the waters of the sea,
But left on shore the sands of history.
Moses spied the distant promised land,
But left the chosen tribes in Aaron's hand.
Moses from on high brought down the Torah,
The world shall come to Sodom and Gomorrah.

2.

Adam, that brave neophyte,
Suffered Eve her appetite;
Solomon, with Sheba on his knee,
Could not forestall the bricked captivity;
Isaiah sang, Ezekiel saw a vision,
All nations shun prophetic circumcision.
The world was cast in anger without end.
The rainbow arcs, its promise to portend.

3.

Jesus hung upon a juniper tree.
He spied across the sea of Galilee
The nations, where they choir and intone
The sacrament of fire and brimstone.

THE POSSIBLE

Tonight, for no particular reason,
The stars are points of meaning.
Bend to touch the possible,
Bend to touch the hem of the dress.

Conceive in its incomprehensible distance
The darkness that is the crown of day,
The fathering, the innumerable atoms,
The single spot in the countless spots of time.

Perceive in the darkness that is our light
The only dance that was ever given,
The woof, the weft of sight,
The thread, the woven phrase.

TO THE MUSE

This is the craft that earned me not a cent,
But schooled me in the book of ill-content,
And taught me in the school of not-so-well,
Because I loved that jade, that Jezebel,
Who eats a man and spits him out like dross,
And counts his life the least part of the cost.
Hail to Euterpe, hail to that fey wench,
Who f---s a man although he has no sense,
But lets another, her true cavalier,
Dance attendance outside on the stair.

SONG

My wife, my belle!
Diaphanous queen
Of all that is seen—
Take my hand!

I will sing you a song
Of our going under,
For our days were comets
That singed the eye.

Your feet were lovely,
O prince's daughter!
Brightest poppies
That lit my days,

Your praise my candles,
Daughter of dust,
Smallest trinket
Lost in the grass.

LOVE SONG

When we pass the gates of the dead,
Will there be lilacs? Will there be roses?
How will we taste the bread?

We are falling
Earthward, and what we see
Is always the earth.
The flesh was eager,
Pronged and budded,
Hungry for life.
You pleased me so,
I did not leave a crumb for others,
Such your generosity.

If we could cleanse the portals of sight,
All would be giving,
For what is held is lost already,
This misapprehension
For which a man would kill.
We are traveling toward a place
Of utmost poverty, deepest cold,
Utter silence, and require
Acts of largest faith, the music of Bach,
Which soared so under your fingers.

When Adam woke from clay,
Was it apple he said, was it quince,
Was it mulberry?

We speak out of a whirlwind,
And what we see a whirlwind,
Trees, the sides of buildings,
The hands we love . . . .

AS YOU NEVER EXPECTED

The ocean rocks on its axis, casting up
Shells, bottles, a piece of polished bone . . .
You wanted life to answer.

It will answer as you never expected,
Out of the mouth of the million toothed possibility,
Into the meadow of bright seed.

The story is started over again,
A phantasmagoria of metamorphosis,
The new star coughing its elements,

Spurs of metal, slivers of cobalt, gobbets of torn flesh.
O, my darling, I cannot continue!
How comely you are in the walks of life,

How worthy of praise! Rain into the ocean,
Leaves from the branching candelabrum,
A piece of tissue paper blown away.

APPOSITE

Half the peach was yours.
And the pear tree of lacelike beauty
Flowering on 83rd Street.
Petals ... petals and foam,
And the wing of the gull
Wheeling over darkened water.

Darling!
The voyage was expensive
And cost us everything.
You gave your life—
Hands, neck,
The poise of the Nepalese girls
With baskets on their heads;
Half yours, the sight of the eye,
An apple shared
That made us happy—
Which is and always was
The world;
The trajectory
Arching out of sight—
The bullseye certain.
This voyage inexhaustible
Was nothing and our own—
Another page of forgotten parchment,
Another testament by st. john.

EPILOGUE

Evening dies, a gull
Wheels over dirty water,
All things taste of ending.
You see behind windows
Men with toothless gums,
Read in headlines
Children shot at the door.
The gears slip, wads of blood
Bob at the jetty—and
Failure is now.

Outside the window
The fritillaries bloom.
The moon is pale as skin
Under an old scab.
Each life is story, legend,
Woven by the imagination,
Unwoven by the night.
Who will sing in his blood
Like water in the gutter?
Who will walk in the gas fires?

The ward is bright with children's drawings.
Death is certain.
I would do Thy will.
When we lie down in darkness,
Who will praise Thee?
Who then will raise Thee?
Who can move this stone?

Power without control,
Direction without purpose,
Intelligence without imagination.
The condom slaps at the pylon.
The eagle screams in its cage.

NORTHWARD

DRIVING NORTHWARD

Driving northward, driving into the night,
Suddenly you know you have driven too far.

The sun has congealed in the west,
It dries at the horizon like blood.

The wind is crying like an animal,
Like a animal that cannot stop.

All is familiar—the pines, the whirring tires,
The stars that shine above you without meaning.

You have finished two thirds of your life, it was easy.
You are driving northward into the night,

Where all is silent, and nothing is unfamiliar.

STARTING YESTERDAY

Starting yesterday, starting
The day before yesterday, starting
Any day, all is happiness.

Light is rising like a mountain,
Like the outstretched feathers of a dove.
Its wings will touch the horizon.

Rest in its illumination,
Which may be illusion after all.
(Have you forgotten your anxiety,

That glove that fit your hand?
Have you forgotten
That catch-breath, your life?)

Your wife is standing by the window,
The wind catches her hair. The wind
Brings the laughter of the children.

RUNNING

How foolish, to be running at your age!
For look! the fields are graced in green.
All is tranquil where you aren't falling
Forward, like a stone. Can you step
Into the light, available as afternoon?
See where the windows burn
With points of flickering dust. Step
Through the familiar, intricate passage
Closing now with salt, closing with tears,
Closing with the passage of the years.

A MIDDLE AGED MAN DREAMING

It is a man sleeping, he dreams the world.
He dreams the beginning before the advent of
The particular, the terrible entropy of fact.
He dreams the sun. He dreams his father.
He dreams the sloppy loveliness of love.
He dreams the marriage of his daughter,
With glasses and flashbulbs and hurrah!
This is his dream, the spinning world,
Blue in the confines of blue space. He dreams his death.
He dreams the failure of ourselves, the
Things we love, the creatures coming and going.
He dreams of existence in a world that's merely sleep.

CARNAL KNOWLEDGE

The wallop of the yellow jacket
Almost knocked you silly. Still,
Because of the children, you pretended
Nothing had happened.

             What had happened?
The hammer blow of the actual, stiletto stab
To the neck, the quicksilver sock
Of surprise. You were stepping
Out-of-doors, the world awash in color,
Eyes turned, women's faces turned—
The weight of the world, which is
The weight of the sun, the weight of
Thigh on thigh . . . Mind dazzled,
Ocean dazzled to the horizon,
Reeling under the provocation
Unforeseen, unprovoked—
It was nothing, darling, nothing,
The world turned upside down:

Love and love and love.

TO THE MUSE

Did you not know that I would write you poetry?
For the poem is no different from the light
That burnishes your hair; and the lines
Are like the flaws and fissures of mortality.
Breathe the perfume of the dust,
Breathe the musk of two hands joining.
Be brave, be silent, be bountiful, for
Passing is swiftness, but its flashing wing
Fans the clover where the small side lies.
This I know, who know all manner of failure
In the exaltation and fever of becoming,
The quick tick along the edge of the arm
That lies beneath you, that writes your name.

LISTEN!

Wind shakes the branches of the hemlock.
Shadows thicken at the base of a tree,
Shadows, and the call of a bird.

The green grass turns white,
And the stones of the mountain
Turn glass, and the sky
Gathers to an attenuated cry
That fills the valley . . .

Over the surface of the past
The branches bend.
You are speaking to the air,
The vacant air. . . Listen!

Love spurts like blood
In the astounded heart!

AS YOU WALK THROUGH THE HERE AND NOW

As you walk through the here and now
You hear the owls in the forest hooting.
You hear the gravel underneath your feet,
The wet slap and slide of snow.
Praise the cold, the hiss of frozen leaves,
The uplifted candelabra of the branches.
In the light of gathering night, the owls
Hoot and howl in the descending snow.

FALLING
DGH

We are always falling
toward earth, but
from such height,
nothing seems to change.
Fields . . . a highway . . .
the curvature of the earth
like a scoliotic spine . . .
the world—that beautiful invention
staring like an eyeball in blue space.
History is what happens below:
a house. . . a room . . .
a small boy in a room
weeping . . . . We are always
falling headlong,
but from such distance,
nothing
seems to change—

and everything is certain.

DECADES
HBH

To have reached you once,
to have reached you,
to have reached you once only,
though you were dead . . . .

The flame thickens,
the fire quickens in the gloaming . . . This
the story that is repeated,
never completed,
the whisper never ending,
the old woman bending, muttering
above the flame . . . .

Fifty years—a puff of smoke,
a spark
rising to extinction.

We have no words to say
what is with us always,
as the eye its seeing,
the ear
the music of its hearing,
our words
a meaning that is always revealing,
always concealing.

To have reached you
once, though you are dead—fog

and the fading eyesight,
lamplight, midnight
and the long unseasoned shaking
of the throat . . .
and this,

unceasing certain eternal love.

IN PACEM

Go down into the place of wisdom,
Be one with that which is,
Be night in the day that is night only.

Be, as it spreads about you slowly,
The primal darkness from which we came,
The oneness without beginning or end.

Let the pleasure slowly steal upon you,
Like summer clouds that pass before the sun.
Become the wheel which is our ceaseless turning.

Become the knowledge that is our only wisdom,
Beginning and end and then again beginning,
In quietness, in desuetude, in peace.

THE WICK

There is a wick,
there is a woof,
there is a whisper.
There is a space
inviolable.

There is a note
before music,
a jewel
beyond treasure,
a tear
lodged at the center.

You the flame,
the wonder,
made thirst,
made hunger,
the light, as in a light burning,
the world turning,
always turning.

This was life, yes,
from the beginning,
believing,
always perceiving,
hearing the cry-
ing the unending
dying, yes,

always—

this was your life.

SPLENDOR

Why should the trees be other than beauty?

For the fishhook snares the lip,
But the trout itself
Is pearline, quicksilver, aquadynamic.
Consider my cat Jeffrey,
Who paws and claws,
And leaps
In fearsome majesty. Consider
The adversary. Consider
The odor of vanilla, which
Your mother gave you.

Hold my hand, do not leave,
As the leaves will not leave for the wind.
Consider the trees, that can tread
All measure of music, dancing and swaying,
For this, for this is splendor.

A WITNESS THAT SOMEONE WAS ALIVE

Here, where this echoes,
a child played on a lawn.
The mountains loomed
above the gathering mist; a red barn
fronted a field; small grasses
lightened the air.

But who was there?
With peanut shells,
with a piece of lucky sea glass,
with silence and the thin brass coins
of betrayal . . . .

What is he saying?
what words? what
sentences? . . . what
today, what
every day? . . .

An arbitrary flight of birds
heading north . . . heading south . . .
heading beyond the horizon.

FOR GABRIEL

My boy, the one the only the now,
and how that can be and how
the fork the spoon and the cow
jump over the moon, and how
that clanging, red invention,
the roaring fire engine,
can please us and amaze
from the outset of our days,
are things for you and me
to ponder, and agree
it's not always easy
to understand, although
the joy of it! and O
the cookie smells that career
from the kitchen stove, my dear,
Mommy and Daddy and Bear,
and the crack in the wooden stair,
light through the window shade,
the rum tum of the parade
of here and now and why,
and the arc of the widening sky,
the do's and don'ts and enough,
(and always love love love)
shall echo throughout your days
in a chorus of all our praise.

AS THE SMALL BIRDS

As the small birds
leap
out of the grass—

startling!
so our words.
And the clouds

pass over,
the light
sifting in columns;

and the grass
turns
like water in your hand.

As the small birds—
the world!
a drop of dew,

a blade of grass,
a leaf of bearded,
long stemmed grass,

bending.

FOR NO APPARENT REASON

Suddenly, for no apparent reason,
summer stands in the door. Yes,

for no apparent reason, although
the wind says sigh, says sigh . . . But why

should the wind say sigh
on a perfect day in summer

when the leaves are a testimony
to the principle of excess? Always

it was you who turned aside, as if
there were a question

you could never answer . . . Now
summer stands in the door

with clouds, with the scent of leaves,
with the scent of swaying flowers.

Walk in the fields, smell the swaying flowers,
let the dancers come together.

SMALL CHANGE

Suds in a drain, rain
Against a window, small change
Left on a bureau. A vase,
A glass, a ring . . . The voice
That wishes to say yes,
But is afraid to say yes, dust
In the pocket of today.

Open the window, let the curtains
Steam in the air. Let the clouds
Float in the mirror. Let the voice
Whisper its name. The black cat
Leaps from the kitchen table.

HE/SHE

He said, one loves the trees.
But in the winter, the leaves
Are pages from a book
That has come to nothing.

Flowers are words, she said.
And the animals, they too are words.
Look! Over your shoulder,
Like summer weather.

He said, there is falling only.
Falling from a great height.
The earth itself is falling
Through the curvature of space.

She said, In the Book of Becoming
There is only becoming,
Being out of Nothing,
Summer out of summer air.

He said, Being rises out of the sea.
It is a rock the shape of the air.
We live beneath the rock, but when we look
We think it is an angel flying.

She said, angels are sparks of seeing,
A revelation of the commons day—
The consummation of eyesight
In the passion of our becoming.

STORY

Rapunzel let down her hair.
The birds of the air
Gathered at the edge
Of her window ledge,
While the soft winds made
A summer serenade.

Rapunzel let down her hair,
The gladsome day
Turned gently at its play,
Turned lithe and debonair
Where the sunbeams crossed
The window's hoary moss.

Rapunzel let down her hair.
While the summer breeze
Gamboled at its ease,
Stirred the golden strands
Beneath her slender hands,
Fair as day is fair.

A tower crowned the croft.
High aloft
Circling lazily
One, two, three
Ravens dropped their cry
Like daggers from the sky.

A tower crowned the croft.
Underneath the soft
Leafage lay a knight,
Still upon his shield.
His horse grazed out of sight
In another field.

A tower crowned the hill.
Rapunzel heard the cry
Of ravens circling by
And her singing stopped
And her mirror dropped.
Her golden brush lay still.

TRISTAN. ISUELT

He said,
the sword that parts us, saves.

And he reached to kiss the place
where touch is happiness,
the spot at the base of the throat
where softness gathers.

He said,
through this valley there flows
a river whose name is silence:
smell the new mown hay.

Outside, snow. A small stain
spread at the corner of the eye.

He said,
when you climb
you come to a place of solitude,
quiet,
the scent of pines . . . .

She said,
close the window,
the swart winds blow.

SONG

You lie down in your bones
The world is a branching tree
There at the tip of the branch
Waits the stinging bee.

The air lifts up its arms
The small bird sighs hello
Under the iron mountain
The children come and go.

Hide in the darkling air
Crouch in the tumbling stream
Rest in the mountain's shadow
Or in the quick sunbeam.

Your hair becomes the wind
Your voice the burning flame
And the eternal valley
Becomes your endless name.

AGAIN

Again, and for the last time,
Speak the unutterable, as in a dance,
The point where the toe pivots. Speak
The place where the world spins.

           The light
Bends like someone who is happy.
The room where you stood
Is fifty years distant,
In the arithmetic of the impossible,
In the absolute.
           Speak
Of the tongue. Speak
Of the ingathering falling
Passing away.
The flowers you saw
Are dust, the merest dust, and
The ineluctable
Turns wayward as a straw,
A floating straw,
Although it remain forever
The inexorable.

BOUNTY

As light through an open window,
Our possibilities. But it happened
The window was only ajar. Yet in the beam
Countless motes, as in a field
The countless summer flies.

                     And you breathe
The odor of apples, blossoms of the air,
Berries of the ripening bush.
August pulls the branch aside—
All measure is bounty poured onto the ground.

These things were offered daily, like water.

Count backward, as when you were a child,
Count the unstoppable sentences,
While through the window, partly ajar,
Cool air chastens the descending night.

CALL IT A DREAM

WHAT IS REAL

i

You are standing in a shaded room,
Outside in the garden,
Sunlight shatters the flagstones.

You cannot know
You will never forget this moment.

ii

You sit by a window,
Sheltered in your mother's arms.
Beyond the window, in the night,

The light says,
Fanny Farmer, Fanny Farmer.

iii

You are in Paris, you are hurrying
To the hospital. As you go,
You count the cracks in the sidewalk,

Thinking,
Remember this! Remember this!

iv

It is a woman, a child, an afternoon,
You are crossing from here to there,
You are pausing for this or that.

Once and once only,
Now and forever,
Thus and thus and thus.

v

You stand on the top of a hill,
It is August,
You are holding your father's hand.

You do not believe your father can ever die.

THE FERRIS WHEEL

Always there is a height—
perhaps a tree, perhaps a hill, or
even a Ferris Wheel. Always
a garden, a plot of green,
as in the Shakespeare garden,
where you paused daily. Always
the weight of being alive, a ball
that stings the hand—as when you found
the pigeon quivering,
half eaten by the dogs.
The eye reached out to touch
a leaf, a strand of hair,
as in music, when the key changes,
and the clouds are parted suddenly;
or in Paris, with the children,
when the Ferris Wheel stopped,
and you saw to the edge of the city.
Always there is this emptiness,
an ache between two points,
a voice that is not you
and yet is only you.
        Speak!
Tell of the need of the tongue. Witness
for impassioned silence. Speak
of the infinitesimal, passing center.

MUSIC

Now that the children have gone,
The house is empty.
Sun streams through the windows,
Shadows lie unmolested.

Outside in the garden,
Where you planted trillium, verbena,
The wind ripples the foliage
Like the edge of a child's pinafore.

And the light is like spun sugar
Falling on the polished floor,
There, by the side of the table,
As in a child's picture book.

Who would have thought
It is the house that has remained?
For the people were disappearing
Like music into the air.

Like notes on the upright piano
That filled the room with music,
Floating out of the window,
Filling the house with music.

CALL IT A DREAM

A word, a voice, a hand.
A shade of light, as in
Applelight, in Edenland.

A flight of stairs. A banister.
A candle on a shelf. A sound
In summer, as in singing

In an Anglo-Saxon alphabet—
The song no louder than
The sound of a child singing.

A mirror, a pitcher of water.
A letter folded.
A letter folded in a bottle.

A life (call it a life).
A dream (call it a dream).
A mother.

HUSH, LITTLE BABY

I took my darling to the edge of goodbye,
And she ran, she didn't look back, and I
Couldn't imagine why she ran like that,
Without a word, without looking back.
It was the World—it was the World and not
The myriad meanings I thought I had begot:
My rhyme, my reason, my sentence, my decree,
A scrap of time, a city block, an obscure pedigree.

I took my darling to the lengthening field,
And she ran across, and her eyes revealed
The thrill she felt to run fast as the wind
Without a thought of looking behind.
I took my darling, and the world said go!
Never look back, never be slow!
Be yourself, be brave, be bold and free,
A minute part of passing eternity.

I gave my love an apple bough,
A diamond ring, a ceaseless vow;
I gave the wind, the scent of rain,
A home that will never come back again;
I gave the infinite, manifold here,
A space to grow through the circling year;
I gave a ring, a rhyming word,
I gave my love a mocking bird.

MOTETS

i

We ate the sun daily,
listening to Mozart
on the patio,
                    although
not as once, when, laughing,
you plunged surfward,
young legs churning,
the weight of the sun

light on your shoulders.

ii

There is gray now in your hair . . .

And those legs that were perfect,
that throat, those hands,
these things
I held in my arms . . . .

Shelter now in this promise,
                    this disappearing,

shelter in this trust.

iii

Now a rope of sunlight
                    falls
from the small balcony of your heart.

A hiss . . . a clash of steel. . . the conductor
is calling from the siding.

You mount
        you turn
                you wave . . .

life is running on the meter.

                    iv

Day is pulled up by the roots,
A lily bleeding.

Count backward
a thousand sentences,
count
a thousand clotted sentences . . .

light
    then night
            then light . . .

life is what it is—

time performs its dark dialysis.

SO SWIFT SO BRIEF

So swift so brief so over.

And you see where the mountains swim
in purple light, the small figures
moving in silence, moving in shadow.
Walk to the end of the block,
pretend that all is eternal;
pretend that the descending night
is but a moment in the cycle of becoming,
an instant in the rhythm of being,
an unending, a returning—

a *you!*

LEAVES

Unless it come as naturally as the leaves . . . .

But what the trees? with branching,
unfolding overarchingness?
with shade in summer, and in winter
song: as sigh of branch,
swing of wind, sweep of soughing bough.

But when the bough must break,
what then will fall? What colors?
What generation of colors
fluttering, fluttering in the wind,
fluttering and falling in the wind.

WORDS CANNOT SAY

Words cannot say
what is given to see
springs up like flame
cools like water
sunset on trees
sheaf of leaves
spruce in the nose
nobody knows
what cannot be said
what is given instead
leaps like fire
circles like air
here—there
everywhere!

THE CEASELESS EULOGY OF SEEING

As you stand on the balcony you see
the acanthus leaves, the curlicues. You see the garden
with bricks and hedgerows and a man
reading a newspaper. You see on the balcony
a young woman at her ease, completely naked . . .
The eye fits perfectly into the footprint
filling with sand, filling with grains of light;
the serendipitous concurrence of the here and now,
the forever-present, certain passing away.

I WENT TO THE WORLD

I went to the world for the keen air beckoned,
And the flowers called from their bending stalks.
If there was a book, what words were written?
And what the sounds of the speaking tongue?

Along the corridor lay miles and miles
Distant, and treacherous as quicksand;
But the sough of the wind enticed like singing,
And moisture like music sweetened the skin.

I went to the world for a voice was calling
Repeating the words of the orient sun,
And a smile spread on the far horizon
Like window-light at break of day.

O, the mistakes that accompanied going,
As if some other way had been offered,
But the roads all pointed down to the valley,
Alive with the sound of rushing streams.

And a voice was calling and what was lovely
Burned on the skin with the hot of the day;
And a scar was scored across the forehead,
A birthmark branded on the breast.

I went to the world for the bread was rising,
And the odor of bread was sweet on the tongue,
And all the stones smelled sweet like baking,
And all the baking would turn to stone.

BEFORE BETRAYAL

Before betrayal, before failure,
There comes the need for failure, betrayal,
The condition for love, the condition for hunger
That set the changeling heart in motion.

The pain that is the condition of all movement
Moves as the child searching for the mother,
Crying out in stations, crying out on platforms,
Turning to strangers, turning away from strangers;

And the heart in its cave calls out for light
While the pulses pant for sweet caresses,
Along the valley, on the hard pressed mattress,
Turning to strangers, turning away from strangers;

And the first mover, love, is also betrayal
Across the valley, along the highway,
Where the trains pant and shunt at the station
Beneath the sun, the condition of being.

Speak now for the sorrow of becoming,
And the love that is the condition of being,
Primal Love, the source of becoming,
Foundation of love, condition of being.

GBH

Now that summer has come
I miss you.
The trees have greened,
their extravagant foliage
baffles sight.
Verde, que te quiero!

Outside, the children's voices
float on the evening air.
Now
you are calling from the window.
Now
it is time to come inside . . .

This is time,
somehow
this is eternity.
Fireflies blink and spurt and extinguish.

Read us a story. Be
the shape of darkness
and goodnight. Be
the sound of possibility
as night comes down.
Be the voice
that is always present. Be
the one that always remains.

I am thinking of summer
I am thinking of fireflies
I am thinking of you.

I CANNOT SPEAK

For—

I cannot speak
so you will not understand.

Go down with me
to the edge of the river,
go
to the edge of the water,
where the plane tree stands.

I stand between shafts of light
in utter darkness,
as if I had not lived for sixty years.

A shade of green,
a splash of orange,
a spot of yellow
flaming in articulation . . .

Words spoken in anger,
words spoken in silence,
words that remain unspoken . . .

I cannot speak
so you will not understand.

THE HEAD FALLS IN THE TUMBREL

Monday, and the head falls in the tumbrel.
The neon lights blink on and off, a black rain falls,
But you are inside, the world is through a window,
The shadows are bars that slip across the floor.
And you recall the faces of your childhood,
Father, mother, brother,
As if a man must live by loss alone.
Mount the stairs, smell the slobber of beer,
Open the door. The letters
All are printed, and the names are printed,
And the sign in the window blinks off and on
And bears your name.

HELLO!

I am glad to be here!
For today, as every day,
sunlight sheathes the window,
and the willow
shakes its illimitable leaves.
Let us praise
a bowl of apples, the
notes on the organ my grandmother played
on Sunday mornings; for
if the world is not a sentence,
it is only because
we cannot stay long enough to hear
the deeprumbled, onrolling distance
of the thunder. Yes,
I am glad to be here
among the intercalated shadows;
and if we reap much benefit
from the daily sunshine
sheathing the window, let us not forget
to speak our eternal name.

sonnet

immovable quiet at the center of being
from which we are in flight as if in fear
as if the secret point of being here
were but to turn our essence into fleeing
and have no more of being or our being
than an incessant hubbub in the ear
as if a truck should slip its second gear
and so go plunging down and disappear

we are the dodgers, we the cheating ones
intent upon this worldly game of chess
in which each player loses more or less
but loves his losses more than what he's won
while all the while the quiet center waits
and neither bargains nor negotiates

LARES

What gods, what tutelary lares
by the ever-flickering hearth?
A clay Jeroboam, a jade turtle,
a Karl's wooden horse
your mother gave you;
from you daughter, an ivory Buddha
squat and serene, whose wisdom
you contravene by loving her.

What place in the cellar,
or on the embankment,
or in the blank bewilderment
of sudden illumination? These things
have been spat out like phlegm,
and what we know
gets sliced up like fish
that slather the hillside.

                    Dear heart,
gather the warmth about you like a shawl.
Set the table,
light the candles,
break the bread.
Sing psalms in a language
known to two only.

THE NATURAL

You enter the natural
as water enters the Gulf Stream,
and the pebbles are laid out
in syllables for reading. The air
is a natural inheritance
that sheathes the sight, as flesh
the collateral skeleton, or blood
the concave of the ear.

Whatever is spoken
has already started on its voyage,
although its beginning
was no more than a word. Utter sentences
that flash like shiny pebbles,
as a man lifts a shell, a child.

But could it be
that the shape of desire was always
this world? The eye, the careful eye,
must hold this otherness
as the nest the fledgling; for surely
what we were really trying to say
was always the shinning pebbles of the real.

LOVE'S BODY

FOR–

As a cat deposits a mouse
by your bedside,

as your slippers are placed
by the door,

as the heart is put
in a tin can

and you will always have the heart, so
take this,

it is yours,
I made it for you.

DESIRE

Once more you set out for the farther shore
Where the waters lap in equanimity.
O, those vatic trees! That heliotrope!
And the sunblanched band of tepid sand
In the saltwater haze of lazy afternoon,
From where a cloud leaps up, a ginger colored bird,
Like a hexameter in an Homeric language.

Give me that fruit to suck to slake my thirst
In the purple heat of noon. O,
Give me that wave. But the scaling waves
Lift hands against the object of progression,
And the whitewater current cracks its whip
Against the human tide; and flashing light
Leaps out in perpetuity against desire.

WHAT IS THE USE

What is the use, the point, the object
of this useless, 19th century thing,
this Love? Regard the clumping birches,
gold against the somber brown of autumn;
the instant when the leaves first fall,
chipped from the inner edge of nothing.
The heart! The heart! that sloppy, deceiving organ,
that objectified distress. These things
are a small locket to wear about your neck.
Quick! Quick! It is love that mounts,
brilliant as the apple-colored dawn.

LOVE'S BODY

Now Love sets out on its journey
like a bicyclist to the corner drug store,
and no one would ever suspect
what's hidden beneath its raincoat.

For if you supposed it was breasts, was belly,
I tell you it is air! The merest air!
It is sunlight along the fur of a cat,
snow in the dirty corners of March.

Love is distorted as a Mercator projection,
and bulges and curves; and we
have composed its history for sheer exuberance
in a Latin language, like a sonata by Poulenc.

Love's body is that glitter in the air,
that fault along the axis that brings in
summer and bright weather.
It is the illusion of existence in a world

that is illusion only, all things
swift and evanescent as soda pop;
the transubstantiation of substance
into flesh, as in a baked potato.

It is the engine of the world
careening toward its precipice:
high air, deep water, quick sound—
the breathtaking dive of becoming!

TO KNOW THE WORLD

Women would have been one way to know the world,
The way they give themselves so bravely,
Like trapeze artists releasing into the void.
I knew the world by mean of a single woman,
Like a man who never leaves Hartford—or like
The swans, entwining their elegant long necks
In the suave persuasions of love.

The earth, they say, is a woman. But
If there is a garden, and if there is a flower,
And if there is a mythology, as in
The mythological gardens of Alhambra,
That flower that garden that mythology is you.
In loving you I came to know the world
In all its incomprehensible mystery, a sacrament
That lasted a lifetime—and forever.

THE THING ITSELF

You lived within the poem
like a man in a house of glass.
It was the woman you loved,
the children, the vocation.
Now the heart clamors for the truth
like a post mortem, and the man
laid out on the slab
is you. Live it all again,
the confusion of the boy,
the arrogance of the adolescent,
the young man with life akimbo,
the middle aged man with middle-aged eyes . . .
live the shape of truth.

           And yet
this shape, this disappointment,
this you—what is it but
the thing itself?—the thing
you always wanted,
the air you breathed,
the world you lived in,
the woman, the children
you loved; what is it but
the words you chose—
the poem itself?

WHAT WAS JULY

It was best to write of winter in July,
For what was summer, which was already passing?
Not the tips of the sassafras, nor
The branches of the arching elm, but
The ranks of recollection, where memory
Pastes it labels to the trunk.
It was better to apprehend in anticipation
The white thin light like frozen milk
Brittle on the tops of glass bottles;
The stick-like poverty of the branches
Broken like discarded toys. But
What had been shaken from winter's rafters
But the thick gold light of summer? What
Was summer but this falling backward,
Where cows are white, and bushes white,
And the thin cold light of midday winter
Is round as berries, bright as berries
Thick on the fat green bushes of July?

LOVE'S BULLFROG

Now love's bullfrog booms at midnight,
and summer lets down her hair.

Why at sixty should you be writing love poems
as if you were a school boy? You thought to write
the poetry of wisdom, but instead
the small nerves of the heart
twitch in finest reticulation.

The moon rises like a poem by Lorca
that has just invented the moon.

The humming bird that lives for a season,
the small moths of a day,
the flies of a summer hour
beat their wings like fans,
and the kite of the sky
rises in the rinsing wind
in deepest blue.

Throw the covers from the bed,
pace across the floor,
stand in the darkened silence.
There is only one woman,
there is only one night,
there is only one poem . . . .

Old masters, old fathers,
moonlight scrapes at the window
like the ragged edge of a can.

WAKE AND KNOW THE THICK MUD

i

Wake and know the thick mud of today
Like the blood of your fathers churning your veins.
And the thin hemorrhage of early morning
Fills the swollen rills with laughter
Where the ink cake dissolves in blackened rain.

ii

Wake and see the branches in precipitous inclination
At the crest of the hill where the path descends,
Under the invisible thumb of necessity
Blown from the mouth of the inconstant passing
Like dragon's breath, like troubled exclamation.

iii

But if this is language, it is only the language
Of a locomotive at midnight at windy distance,
For what is passing is irrevocable
In the dim recess of the inconceivable,
Like an umbrella left at the back of a closet.

iv

The privilege of knowing, the privilege of becoming,
Stand upright on tip-toe on a windy pinnacle,
Balanced like an egg on a windy pinnacle;
And all the creatures sneeze and trumpet and cry
In the unceaseable wonder of being alive.

WHERE I HAVE NEVER BEEN
DGH

Where I have never been, where the current
Cuts the cliffs, and the rocks
Are ochre and sandstone; in a place
Where spirit cries out in poverty, you chose
(Having soared beyond our reach) a spot
Where the heart is alien and at home.

I remember a day
When our mother was younger than we are.
Your beauty wowed me! How proud I was!
Running before you in a race you could never win,
And have long since outdistanced.
Reach back to me across the love
That seems ephemeral, and must be eternal,
And is the only mercy we can conceive.

The canyon folds its shadow,
An eagle launches above a landscape
Of rock and sun and dust.
Gather me, Brother, into eternity,
Where the coldness is so great,
And where alone we can embrace.

THRENODY

On a windless day a threnody,
not from the throats of birds,
nor from the grass, whose scent
graces the air, nor from
the highpassing clouds
that part and gather and disappear,
nor from the wind, hardly astir,
that touches with light heaviness
the cheek, the hand.

The melody of insects
flickers in the grass, the endless dream
of summer. Innumerable noises
whir and chug and whisper
in the orchestra of becoming—
the orchestra of death.

Beneath all appearance
there lies emptiness, blankness
beneath seeing, loneliness
beneath love—although
how this can be
no one has explained.

What we see is only an island,
a clutch of bird,
a distant headland—the place
where, in the end,

we find our happiness,
or not at all.

Awake, as a man awakes
who finally understands
that all he ever saw
was always, truly, wonder.

LIGHT THAT FELL

What is air? What are children?
What the hunger you breathed?
For the light that falls on water
remains, although the water
passes forever. And the woman
leaning above your daughter,
is long dead, and is a ghost
above your daughter, who is
a ghost as well . . . .

The sacrament you ate,
the year of happy living,
the woman, the garden, the child
have ascended into the nostrils
like smoke,
and will not return. Cry
for the rafters burning
the child departing,
the wound unhealed . . . .

The lip of the cup,
the lip of the rain,
the lip of the passing moment

disappearing.

SMOKE

These things that served their purpose,
a street, a vacant field,
the noise of children playing . . . .

              It was you
who always turned aside—and
not like the seasons,
which come again,
but like the smoke
that hangs an instant in the air,
that hangs . . . that hangs . . .
then disappears.

            It was you
who served, yes, gladly, although
you cannot imagine how,
though you would do it again,
yes, would do it all again,
gladly . . . .

         And the smoke
hung like a fire that has burned all night,
you watched it on the hillside,
now copper, now orange, now red,
burning all night until at morning
there was nothing—only
charred and distant fields,
and smoke,
and the insistent odor of smoke.

GODDESS

But surely
the wings of the goddess
were lovely
with hair swept back
like a dancer
with wings
swept back
at the top of the stair
there
where she waited
whose purpose
was always
only
to say

Now!

FINAL LETTER

Now love commences
its strange contortions, like fish
tossed on the shore; and
the golden girls cry out to—what?

Summer sits like a king,
but in its regency, death.

Your eye surveys
the tangle of summer,
in love with the color green:
instances of what was always right
about the project of breathing.

And you recall
the lives you witnessed, like
so many run-on sentences that now
have stopped forever.

Summer sits like a king,
but in its regency, death—
the death of the leaf,
the death of the individual.

The kids commence their chants of love
in a scripture not to be taken seriously,
letters from a book you read a hundred times
but never comprehended . . .

Write now
the gargled sentences, the lovesick slobber,
like a bottle passed from mouth to mouth. Write
the dithyrambic hoopla, the incessant,
the unstoppable poem . . . Is this
your final testament, your final letter?

LIKE A FLAME

As a sailboat
points into harbor

and takes delight
in the suave sway of the weather,

so the soul selects its own,

a dress in summer, a breeze
in the cool heads of the flowers . . . Thus

when like a flame
she entered

brightness
lighted the eye.

FROM A LETTER

I only wanted to say
the hills were purple,
mist gathered in valleys,
a child was singing—
or perhaps was only humming,
you were walking beside me, rain
lit on your face . . . .

                  Something
has to come from all this living,
the countless days that offered their colors,
the innumerable clouds that passed above us,
the unending ways we had to know
that we were happy. . . .

SPOONS FROM A DRAWER

Salt from a shaker
spoons from a drawer
light on a cut-glass goblet
a peony, a violet
the limbs of the swimmer
heavy with ocean
the lungs
aching for breath
the one who said no
and turned away
and the one who said yes
forever—
why do you ask
and why do you cry out
where at the corner
light goes down to darkness?
and you recall
a polished table
a chair
the stem of a flower
and at the tip
a rose, bending.

DISTANCE

Now in the warmth of afternoon
your mother is nursing her child.
The only sound is the creak of the rocker,
the tick of the clock, the burr of traffic
outside the window.
                Motes of dust
dance in the air. You are four. Your eye touches
her breast her skin her hair . . . Your brother is wrapped
in babyhood, he will never remember
this instant, this afternoon . . . .

                Sun descends
from another window. Your brother
is long dead, your mother. Warmth
is elsewhere. Touch
the inconceivable, the
the skin of the departed. Touch
the irrevocable. Touch
your mother nursing her child.

THE MUSIC OF TIME

Now the heaviness of air
squats like destiny
and the porous lungs
suck up living.

The lip of the rain
moistens the leaf.

Sunlight glitters
and the paludes
fill up with scum.

And all is famous
for an instant
      in the sun
and the sun
for an instant
      in time
and time
for an instant
      in eternity

and the music of time
blossoms on the raspberry bush.

TO WAKE BESIDE YOU

To wake beside you like oxygen
beside hydrogen in the compound
that sustains all life. To see
sun in your hair as a natural expression
of light out of darkness, life
out of nothing, love out of
the unceasing cravings of the heart. To know
your absence as the deprivation
of all purpose, like an animal
sick in a corner; to feel your presence
like heat through the capillaries,
the thought of you the flame
round which we gather, as the dead
gather around human blood. Heart
that sustains, tongue that nurtures,
hand that proffers water, world
opens before you as before
the wide-eyed grave-eyed child, who stops
to wonder at each flutter
in spontaneous, immediate confirmation.
These things are offered daily, as
the pump of lungs, the knock of the knuckle
guarding the wedding ring, the cat
attendant at the foot of the bed,
who trusts that soon the small mountain
curled beneath the covers, will stir,
and life will spring into meaning.

poem

Now autumn crimsons the trees
with its diminishing vocabulary.

Shadows lengthen. The legs
that once were perfect

submit to imperfection.
The world submits to silence.

IN THE PHOTO

In the photo I can see the child
Standing in a puddle of misapprehension,
Though what is dear about the child
Retains one's momentary attention.

I see the boy in all his sweetness
And all his trouble, without a clue
How to add the columns of living,
Like one who can't add two and two.

I see the eyes in all their confusion
Without a notion about the pain
Which will fall like rain and lightning
Only to rise and fall again.

I know the child, I know the secret
Like a signpost in a Grecian town,
I know the road-block of his future
Like a man hung upside-down.

I am content to be that child,
Tongue tied, shy, confused of wit,
Whom all my life I've tried to bury,
As a dog a bone when he's through with it.

YOU WANTED TO WRITE A POEM

You wanted to write a poem.

For the world fits into a poem
as a cupcake into a boy's appetite.

The old disappearing act
eats up your youth, your fatherhood,
and all you had,
and the blackened pages
rise in the updraft, carrying words
that served their purpose ...

Sing, bird, sing in the bursting bush,
though you are only a robin;
sing the return of spring,
as your mother once taught you.

You stand before the people you love
condemned of folly, as if
as a boy, as a man, there had been
a another road you could have followed.
Age now looks at its face, its hands, and recognizes
the face of the man, the boy.

You wanted to write the world.

Mother, child, wife,
incarnations of the life

you clutched
but could not hold;
a song you used to sing
before your voice went hoarse.

Sing, old man, sing
in the only poetry you still can sing,
in a passion of praise and failure
in universal celebration.

THE BUDDHA THAT SITS
IN MY GARDEN

Not the act of loving,
nor anything
that lives, that grows,
that dies, for this,
for this is error.

And the mistake
cried out to you,
you held it in your arms,
it was a child,
a woman,
a flower.
The green sap
drove in the blood,
it moved on legs
that were almost perfect—
this untruth for which
a man would die. . . .

El delito mejor

Cold eye
of truth,
stern eye
of wisdom.

Death.

Love sat
under the bodi tree,
it was warm
it was young
it was breathing . . .
you reached to touch her hand,
you brought it to your lips
in love
in gratitude

in error.

COMMENDABLE

Now the white flowers
glow in evening shallow,
and the thought of what she was
returns. For look!
the mortal is mouthchanging,
breathchanging, like air.

I would praise the place behind her knees,
smooth as sea glass; her neck,
a turret of light; her thighs,
warm as summer petals—although
all was careening out of sight
like a taxi . . . .

          Sing now
the certain purpose, the
caring tongue; uprightness
like a spine; love like a muscle
pumping to the extremities;
sing the butterfly wing
where the humanly commendable
fluttered for an instant, and praise
echoes before dying.

BLESSING

Now the gold bugs sing in the rafters
and your only life
slips through your hands like water.

Sing the things that change:
hair that fell in a cloud,
house that stood for a year,
light that rose like a flame.

Sing what is permanent
in a world without permanence, holy
in a place without wholeness:
the silk of summer
glistening in opulence.

O, ghosts! O, fathers!
insist, insist,
as the rider holds the horse between her thighs,
and the ancient rabbi
chants the letters of the blessing.

BOOK III

(2006 – 2009)

PARTS OF THE WORLD

DÜRER

What was that gilded lie
but life? An apple on a bough,
a story that gets repeated,
a hand that clutches
the tree of knowledge ...
It was life itself,
the woman you loved—yes,
especially the woman; the beam
in your eye, yes, especially
the beam. It was surcease of pain
in a world that is pain only,
a mystery embodied in flesh,
the girl beneath the date-nut tree.
It was love in its metaphysical pretensions,
a way of being, a woman
with a flame of goldbrown hair ...
It was a man standing beside her,
his fingers grasping a twig,
the leaves that covered their sex,
the polished alabaster of
her breasts, the apple that she held,
the serpent on the branch—
yes, especially the serpent,
coiled, and gilded in truth.

DÉJEUNER SUR L'HERBE

This picnic on the grass, this dejeuner,
what is it but the common moth? And what
this plein air but an artist's trick? What
this Manet which set the bourgeoisie howling
like a water closet that won't stop?
what this picnic but—celebration!
The girl at ease with her nakedness,
the white flesh tanning like marshmallow, the men
pedantically explaining something or other,
the women waiting patiently to be divvied up
like cards on a Saturday evening; in the background
nature—and in the foreground,
nature too, for what are we but nature
with a little clothing? (As if a dog should say
"pass the Champagne," and then should add,
"my good man!" for emphasis!) Yes,
with our ingestion and egestion like a hydro-pump,
our ceaseless gas exchange, birth copulation
death, like the joke about the hunchback
who didn't want anyone to know
he was a hunchback . . . our need for sex,
a flag that rises and falls, rises and falls,
our need for love . . . .

A picnic on the grass with a condom,
a sausage, a hymen burst like a blister;
pissing behind bushes, the odor of excrement
rank on the fingers, the groan of sex,
the sigh of exhaustion, the sound of invocation

(as if any god could care less!)
the scrimmage of love between two humans
caught like muskrats in a flood,
necks held rigid above the water;
and what can save them (for
nothing will save them) except
illusion—a picture, a poem—the belief
that the heart can pump can pump
a reservoir, a puddle, a life.

TWO

If God is love, He must feel, as we do,
The lack of that which love directs us to;
Like hunger or desire, so is love
The want of that loved thing we're hungered of.

Two make one, one has need of two,
So the heart is fractured through and through;
Nothing is whole; wholeness is a word
That plasters up the hole of the absurd.

It is us living mortals, it is men
Whom love moves like a torrent; even when
The wound seems staunched, the pain is living still,
And drives the beating organ of the will.

Love is need turned inward to the heart
That's cleft in two, like fruit that's split apart.

GOLD

The fact that we are living in a body
Contributes to our state of being shoddy,
Just as a man who's tossing in the ocean
Is mindful of the sickness from such motion.

And yet the body ought to get its due
For taking one and turning it to two,
A kind of alchemy within our fold,
That takes the fleece and changes it to gold.

PAIN THAT WON'T DIE

The grackles have nested under the window,
we hear them squabbling like neighbors,
you knock against the wall to stop their noise.
Spring is a candle of bees wax held in your hand,
a single candle with the early scent of heat.
I reach out in the dark, but there is no candle,
only the uproar of voices,
shriek of siren, grind of engine, squeal of racing tires . . .

"The sun gets in your blood,
an afternoon, a sheet kicked to the floor;
your hear the small boats in the harbor
rocking, your clothing
kicked to the floor."

"Why did I marry you? Why did I ever marry
such a child?"
                You hear them on the terrace,
she bent forward, her breasts
brushing his hand—
the prow of a ship cutting water . . . .

The beauty that she was returns,
a candle at morning, I mean our spring,
I mean of course our youth. . . . Her body
like a question mark under the sheet . . .
clothing strewn on the floor,
toys on the floor, our world
a sand castle strewn on the floor.

The grackles are building under the window,
the male flies back and forth, we hear
their squabbles like a marriage that who won't last . . . .
Waves where we walked by the shore,
your hand a candle I could always find,
it was always beside me, there at night beside me,
like the twisted sea weed where we walked,
scented like bees wax, and slowly burning.

SHORTS

i

I do not count the days of the week
Which are irrelevant, so to speak,
To this life that fell on me
Like a sac of bricks in a factory.

I do not count the months of the year
Though such insouciance may appear
Provoking to the powers that be
That loll about in eternity.

I sport a cravat, I comb my hair
And seem as if I hadn't a care
But driving fast and eating well
And wishing my neighbors safe in hell.

ii

The long descent
from sacrament
is expense
of experience.

Thus is crowned
in muck and piss
the mortal folly
of genesis.

iii

Women of all varieties,
in all the known societies,
are partial to the sex called male
and wouldn't give a dead rat's tail
once the day has turned to night
for proprieties dites polite;
nor in truth do they regret
any ensuing interlude,
whether by word or internet,
conducted strictly in the nude.
In this they differ not a span
from the creature known as man.

iv

All I'm really useful for
Is writing verses—more and more
Blood and guts spilt on the floor.

v

We eat death on the installment plan,
Daily digesting what we can;
The rest we store inside of us
To clog the stomach and esophagus.

A LINE BY CAVAFY

So much he gazed on beauty,
So much he gazed,
That the objects of the world
Blazed beneath his gaze,
The objects of this world.

But mostly it was the limbs of women,
The beautiful limbs,
Mostly it was the beautiful limbs of women
That blazed beneath his gaze,
So much he gazed on beauty.

CARIBBEAN

i

The Caribbean swelled beneath us—
venereal soil
lit with picture-post-card incandescence.

The lizard froze to the wall,
the sun
nailed its shield to the door,
the ocean
hammered its tom-tom, and our bodies
lay at ease,
riding at anchor.

ii

The ocean stretched behind us
strewn with islands,
palm trees, shacks
torn up in tornadoes . . .
straw, fronds, debris—
a cornucopia of possibility
resolved like waves
in one direction only.

iii

Forty years,
the flick of the sandpiper's wing . . . .

iv

The woman you love
recedes to the horizon . . .
Ripples and ribbons
raked by the wind,
blown in from the sea,
cobalt, aquamarine,
magenta . . . waves,
tears, words . . .
the midnight cry
of the alligator.

v

What is love?—is it
the bilateral split
where the sperm
halved the egg? or
the cicatrix
where the scalpel
carved the flesh? or
is it (as in the parable
by Plato) the cleft
where lightning
split us in two
down the middle?

MANET

In Manet's great picture of the picnic,
his favorite model, Victorine Meurent,
sits at ease in her birthday suit,
regarding the viewer with abstracted indifference.
Her lovely, unspectacular body
forms an almost ninety-degree angle,
one of several geometric figures
around which, in dazzling technique,
the master has constructed his work.
What the viewing eye beholds
is a healthy, stark-naked young woman,
her clothing strewn on the grass,
while two fully dressed gentlemen, legs akimbo,
sit locked in the orbit of her nonchalance.

In Olympia, the same Victorine
stares at the spectator with haughty disdain,
as who should say, "What did you expect?"
or perhaps, to the women
accoutered to the hilt in their Victorian
whalebone—"Tu quoque!" (The famous cat
in the lower corner is to remind us
that the magic of sex is always black.)

         One painting is executed
in dark greens, browns, immaculate blue (the dress
thrown on the grass) and the pale verdigris
favored by Manet for Victorine in the buff. Olympia offers
"harmonies of blacks, grays, and whites

enlivened by some strong or subtle notes," including
the now infamous greenish white
of Victorine's maculate nudity, which
to the cognoscenti, proclaims "je ne suis pas une nue!"

The two poles of the pictures are united
by a body no more spectacular than birdsong
or rainlight. Dejeuner sur l'herbe!
the lost paradise where gentlemen in morning coats
bore a naked beauty silly, while she
dreams away the painter's endless hours.
Olympia! the tribute of flowers delivered by
Stevens' negress to a naked fille
basking her indifferent beauty between customers.
Ah, Manet! at the center there invariably appear
the bourgeois paraphernalia, flowers, a naked woman,
the world of nature at ease
in female resplendence:
the perennial, impossible struggle of art
to make sense out of any of it.

POEM

Today there are no trees,
The branches are filled with emptiness.

How can I speak? How can I speak
In a language without revelation?

This is the word, this the syllable,
That breathes the empty air.

The house is empty. The day is cold.

THE POEMS OF NIGHT

I wrote the poems of light,
verses of hibiscus, tea leaves, clover,
bird song in the sun-drenched trees,
an olive branch, a peacock's feather . . . now
I will write the poems of night.

I will write the serpent on its rock
hissing, the yellow eye
darting in warning, the forked tongue
spitting its poison. I will write
the tablature of Apollonian flesh
carved in the unpardoned figure of man,

the unforgiven, the unforgivable.

THE POETRY OF WISDOM

I wanted to write the poetry of wisdom,
harvests in the fields, mountains
soaring in C, the golden, the unimpeachable light . . . Instead
a cur in the pit with teeth bared, its ear
half eaten by the dogs . . . .

                    Isn't it time
that something came from all this living?—where
the mot juste, the hard-earned phrase,
the statue carved in classical ease? Where
the balance that rises and falls, rises and falls,
like the breasts of the beloved,
the heartbeat of naked truth?

TRUTH

When we are dead, when we can know the truth,
Will we then know the Truth? or will we rather
Turn away, knowing that human truth
Is not worth knowing? . . . I will turn away,
Knowing that truth is not the Truth,
Not even the human truth, but is a truth
That wears man's smudge, and bares
Man's dirty face. For love
Is truth enough, given
Not for show, mere human show,
But meant to stay and grow into that love
Which surely shall suffice.
And therefore when we know,
Truth is no surprise, although
Heartache true enough. But love
Is what is truth in otherwise.
So when we are dead, the truth we wish to know
Is evident, self-evident, and we will know.

THE SUPREME NATURE OF LOVE

The supreme nature of love
cries out like roots
in alluvial soil. This
we observe in children,
language, and
the heart itself, an organ
of metaphor, a bridge
traversing troubled water.
Love declares itself
in clouds, roots, dandelions,
the whiskers of animals, the
sex of women, and
(I suppose) the blind rootings
of the male. But the end of love
is Love, as in
ancient cartography,
the ocean that upholds
the terrestrial globe. And so
the poor heart yammers,
trusting like a baby,
as flowers turn to the sun
in the primal, phototropic tug
that starts all motion,
the one, the supreme,
the presiding X.

letter

if now
i dripped down like wax,
and smoke
were the only answer,
who is to say
I had not loved
my burning?

THE COUNTRY OF SMALL GRASS

i

What eyeball fell among the grass?
What sight among the daisies?

ii

Now you know again
the distance that divides you from yourself.

iii

Where the mind assumes love's gamble,
everyone must lose.

iv

Flesh is vanity, that cometh like the grass
and is blown away.

v

See how the sky is broken into clouds
and handfuls of flying birds.

vi

What is beauty but a pasture with a horse?
What August but sex and death?

vii

The eye surveys the field,
a valley encircled by a narrow horizon.

POSTCARDS

i Honeymoon

June. The heat already up
in the smeared, sweltered streets
of Manhattan . . . Only
a woman walking a dog, a man
walking a dog—and
you and me! Youth
is crossing Fifth Avenue
with a world-class beauty on your arm!

The shaded rooms of 970
were perfect for love
when one was
twenty! . . . strength
was in my arm, my hand,
my eye, which
couldn't get enough of you,
and never has! . . . Secrets?
how could there be secrets?
starting life together,
inventing life together . . .

        That afternoon
the airplane banked into
the smog of Manhattan . . . Next stop,
Paris! What luck!—you,
my one and only wife, this
our one and only honeymoon!

ii Chenonceau

At Chenonceau you shivered beneath my hand
in the June night, the *son et lumiere*
lighting the chateau like a wedding cake.
Dew glittered like champagne as I held you—
the fisherman who had pulled the mermaid
out of the sea! . . . At sixteen
we were steadies, at seventeen
lovers, at twenty,
married. Now we stood
in the valley of the Loire, in the late June night,
in the fabled realm of France,
where the vast uncountable stars
flashed above us like warnings.

What do I remember of Chenonceau
but the cold, the stars, the glitter of dew—
your small shoulder
under my hand? Later
I sped through pitchblack night,
twisting on back roads
as treacherous as life—
twenty and immortal, the girl I loved
beside me in the dark—life
beside me in the dark.

iii Milano

Milano, where the thin gray light
sifted like rain through the railway station,
steam rising, wheels hissing, passengers
pushing for exits—and then
Italy! enchanted ground,
life before us like a thousand stations
in a thousand destinations, with you
in a dress, or wearing slacks, with
hair in a braid, or loose, or pulled aside,
small mouth and perfect teeth,
legs perfect and neck
the neck of the swan!

How you took me in hand,
ordering breakfast in your schoolgirl Italian:
café macchiato; pane con marmalado!
Perfect hour! a golden ring
lost in the grass (your great aunt's earrings
lost the first time you wore them—
remember?) You conducting us on the El
to the hostel you had provided, the city
billowing beneath us like steam . . .

One day for la Scala, that drip-castle cathedral
of marzipan, the glass Arcade,
where we wandered like Hanzel and Gretel,
hand in hand; The Last Supper,
faded and monumental as a cave painting . . . Outside,
pollen dizzied the air; in a week

it would poleax me with hay-fever.

The next morning, Florence!
you already heavy with our child . . .
What is life but a series of cities,
hotel rooms, revelations? names
on a map where we walked
or talked or quarreled . . .
Glancing over my shoulder,
I thought you were following, although
you had in fact lapped me already! . . . I followed
blindly down the rabbit hole,
our days a series of letters
posted and sent away—this one
a love letter for you.

AFTER DEATH

After death, in that still place called death,
in that labyrinth of time untimed,
that unthinkable reality of the unreal, where
unhousseled ghosts move bodiless as smoke;
in that bald place of wordlessness
where green is neither green nor gray
but unspeakable unsayable absence,
as after an infarction, when the x-ray
is black as ink; after death,
in that pseudo-realm, the half-mind
moving in otherness—how then will I
find thee, know thee, hold thee,
after a lifetime of loving thee, like wind
in the summer trees, or sky light
in the blue reflection of a lake? How
speak about your worthiness,
a daily increase, as coral
accumulates its monumental beauty
by infinitesimal accretion, or the constant drip
that carves to edificial statuary
the towering, awe-inspiring stone.
Here is the place for love, where bone
lies homed in body, not in the loam
of ash and clay. After death,
in that bad place called death,
how tell thee my love, the way
peaches scent the air
with August aroma, or you
the daily lifetime of our life?

IMPOSSIBLE TO SAY

Summer closes its eyes. But
what was summer
but innumerable leaves
smoking to nothing? What the sun
but ignorance repeating its name?

Something is broken . . . a ratchet
at the center of somewhere . . . But what of love,
that four letter word?—It too
is broken, its parts
rusted like nails . . . The hero
was a ninny, the heroine
a woman he had never known . . . .

Summer closes its eyes. The poems
sleep in their notebooks, the words
fall to the floor. The act of love
still throbs, an unstoppable
hemorrhage, an unaccountable
pronouncement in a language
close to gibberish . . .

                From a bush
a brown thrush sings. Pollen
floats in the air. The book
rests on the table. The pages
are closed, the epic
was never written . . . .

THE PLEDGE

Was it a kiss, my darling,
Was it a pledge,
Those words you told me when
We were but twice times ten,
When the panting heart
Was split by love's first dart?

Repeat, repeat, my dear,
That now far distant pledge,
Those words you promised then
To mean forever when
The heart was still on fire
With twice-times ten desire.

FIELD FORCE

How utterly unfair! As if
you merited from this lucky stiff,
after all these years, decades,
anything but love and praise
for being what you are, became,
not changing, staying just the same,
the glue that held us tight together
in fair as in the foulest weather,
though this is much too tame and bland
to make a body understand
how much I leaned and leaned to you,
driven and driven through
by the field force of your being,
seeing, unseeing,
as the world went reeling by,
the light, the firelight of my eye.

I say that mortal human clay
must bend to harsh necessity
as moth to lamp, as twig to flame,
intention to word, knowledge to name;
I, who have always tried to say
in one, and then another way,
for years and years, nay decades,
all that deserves unending praise,
crowning your much-loved, mortal brow
now as forever, then as now.

PARTS OF THE WORLD

i

The world lay all about us in parts
that could never be fitted together.

                In California
the parts were hills, clouds, horses
small as the toys you played with as a child.
Young women lay about you, a basket,
a half-empty bottle of wine . . . Our lives
lay about us, mysterious, unknowable,
disappearing into the dark; a sentence
that could never be completed, a circle
that could never be squared.

ii

Memory
where is your door?

a river
a meadow
swollen with light
eyes
sifted with gold
the odor of sage
the aroma
of crushed thyme,
an arm
beneath your head
a hand . . .

sounds of children
singing
underground
a sail
a distant shore
words you have heard before
a checkered dress . . .
light in darkness.

Reaching,
you brought the earth
slowly to your lips.

iii
To know the world
is not to love it
although
to love it is to know it
after a fashion—
a horse
galloping on a hill,
the earth, the sky
a particle of light
stuck in the eye
a wife, two daughters
a narrow plank
over troubled water . . .

parts of the world.

THE LAND OF UNKNOWING

AFTER AIKEN

Music I heard with you was more than music,
And bread I broke with you was more than bread,
For what is bread if not an earthly music,
Or music but a kind of heavenly bread?

But you yourself were like the complex music
By which we learn to tread our darksome way,
As if the masters with their heavenly music
Could only body forth our earthly way;

So that the constant playing of our music
Is filled with World, and with its daily bread,
Which turn the head like wine with earthly music,
But not the Way, which offers different bread.

And yet the daily music of your love
Was Bread and Way and Music sure enough.

UNKNOWING

Looking down into the waters of the self,
Looking into that place
From whence there issues only other space
Where eye cannot reach, mind go,
Nor hand know
The contour of that otherness; thinking
Of the continued falling,
Which is that looking,
Time passing, mind unknowing,
In the growing ignorance of its knowing;
How can I know and how can I ever name
What is forever fleeing
Into an unknowing, so that one is always leaving
The self for a different self, the safe
For a hidden and more dangerous place,
Outside the harbor where the sailboat rides?

Love itself is an unknowing,
A perpetual growing—or ungrowing,
(O, the ceaseless falling
Into the endless waters of unknowing!)
A glowing in mid-distance, just before
The place where our short eyes can see no more,
A darkward and abysmal farther space
Impenetrable even to the belovèd face,
Who leaves us there, who turns her back and goes
Eurydice-like, but up the other way
Into the sun-lit fields of common day.

O, let it not be said
That there is other ending;
For love is the wager that we make
On trust, that the belovèd face
Is not a cloud of our unknowing,
Floating dissolving going,
But a staying with our going,
A falling in place together. O,
Love in the depths with nowhere to go,
Dive like a dolphin, swim swim!
For nowhere else is home
And no one is at home
But the light, the bright and shining sight you bring
And the hard uncertain song you learn to sing.

THE PROCESS OF LOVING

In the process of loving
there is only loving
though sometimes that loving
seems like unloving
breathing is loving
the source of our being
though loving and Being
are stricken asunder
mystery, wonder!
stricken asunder
from source of our Being
the true source of loving
loving my wonder
is loving your being
although all true Being
is hidden in seeming
loving is being
asserted in wonder
my wonder in loving
the source of your being
the thing itself, Being,
there in your being
the object of wonder
the source of our loving

LINES

Though God is spirit, nature
Is also God's true nature
And fills the plenum such
That God proves overmuch
Here and there and there
Yet truly a Nowhere
So that this ceaseless flux
Is constant paradox
A negativity
Conferring certainty
And thus in this respect
Transcending intellect
But offering inspection
Above mere intellection
With freedom to declare
Its center everywhere
And yet a point from whence
There's no circumference
For Spirit soaring free
Knows no such boundary
Except by that supplied
By its unbound Inside.

THE DIALECTIC OF THE HEART

The dialectic of the heart
Describes the syllables of love; a molecule
In the great improbable bonding
Of that-which-is; the indissoluble,
Unlikely coming together
Of this-and-that—unaccountable
By any statistic, since nothing
Has to be, neither
The tip of the finger nor
The swirl of the galaxy. It is
The human code, the every day,
The sonnet in the language of genetics,
The salad from the garden of becoming,
The single pronouncement in the wind
That blows that blows that blows.

MOTETS

i

Where raindrops lit the grass,
Fire! And the opal light
Shone like a stone on your finger.

Love's loss, love's profit

Shone like a stone on your finger.

ii

In Paris,
With traffic under the window,
With cars and horns under the window
Blaring on the side street—the French windows
Opened against the heat; in Paris,
Where we spoke our name . . . .

iii

Of pleasure most folks never get enough;
Dogs return to vomit, men to love.
The Jews are an old nation, and the Chosen,
Although most people like to bash their nose in.
Christ hung on the cross, yet Christianity
Isn't keen to give up its profanity.
Christ hung on the cross, yet old St. Paul
Conjured cotton candy out of gall.
Christ hung on the cross, yet the nations
Still delight in beating a man's face in.

Kicking and punching is the game we play,
O, pray for us upon the great Pay Day.

iv

Archetypal sun, the primal light,
Magnificent maker of eyesight,
Manifests for all to see
The face of the hidden deity.

v

In the glitter of the night
Spanish Calderon had it right,
All that is, all that seems,
Is but the conjunction of two dreams.

love

was the language of her body:
length of limb, fullness
of breast and thigh,
fall of sun on hair—
loss would be
tantamount to dumbness,
as if tongue
clung to the roof of the mouth.

Walking,
holding a hand or
nipple . . . where
that summer
that zinged like a tennis ball?
Light
that lit that page,
wherewith shall that light
be lighted?

What banister
in the shiver of night? the
point of insight
acid in the eye,
the vision of time
blind in the sun . . .
where now

the language of youth,
the language of love,
the language of misapprehension?

IT IS UNWISE TO BELIEVE IN SUMMER

It is unwise to believe in summer, as
It is unwise to believe in chastity, only
Opposite. It is unwise to trust
The pullulating of insects, the croaking
Of summer frogs, who from their bogs
Sing love refrains throughout the summer night.

It is unwise to trust the words that say
I will love you today, every day
Forever, which is a long long time
And fits more neatly into rhyme
Than in duration, day-by-day,
Which is quite long, and not mere child's play.

It is not creditable to take at face value
The frogs that go a courtin', as Granny sang,
Who now lies under a tree, in what used to be
Our parent's home, who've now gone home
To Paradise, or some such place,
Leaving my bother and myself to sell the place.

It's not to be believed that summer days
Breed chastity in summer hours
Nor that the potent fickle powers
Employ a human vocabulary,
Which says a lot, and means a lot,
Like whipped cream on confectionary.

PEACH

Certain it was no apple but a peach
That Eve and Adam noshed on each with each,
Giving themselves the bellyache that we
Inherit in the guise of history.
For apples though nutritious are not quite
So suave to taste or pleasing to the sight
As peaches are, and that's the reason why
A girl is called a peach who holds the eye,
And reddens as if blandishments offend her,
Though in conclusion stoops to human gender.
And this explains why Adam, having bitten
Into that fruit, remained forever smitten
By the taste, dazzled by that girl
Who threw him topsy-turvy in the whirl
Of history, falling on his face,
And ordered by an angel, in disgrace,
To quit forever our ancestral place.
What he won was Eve and that sweet fruit
That changed our inner essence at the root,
And so forever peaches keep the savor
Which calls to mind that paradisal flavor.

TREES ARE FLOWERS

Now in summer, when flowers are bushes
And bushes are trees; when trees
Are flowers sent from a lover's hand,
Enchanting but not to be trusted, like bees
That weave in summer weather, floating,
And stinging the child's hand (and I said,
Be still, be still, it will not hurt you!);
What can hurt you in the trees
That take their ease in summer, as if summer
Were a bonus in fat dollars and not
A stinging bee? Yes, now, in summer,
When summer can never be over and August
Is a bonus for an opulent banker,
The leaves of the trees all shake
Like the dollars a banker will make,
And the children have all gone away,
Some to play and some to go away and some
To die, like small birds that fall from the sky
In winter, frozen by winter weather, and far,
So far from summer, when trees are flowers.

FOR AN INSTANT

For an instant summer stayed in the eye,
Yes, for an instant, as a sail
Passes, or as light
Polishes the table top. But who,
Yes who, polished the table top?
As if a word should float before you
And then disappear! But how, you ask yourself,
Yes how could such a word just disappear?
As if a tense just disappeared, a season,
The odor of honeysuckle,
Moonlight along the edge of mud?

It was the Mother who polished the table top,
Who disappeared; it was the Mother
Who stayed an instant, who stayed,
Who stayed, and then—disappeared!

                                        Summer
Stayed an instant in the eye,
Bloodshot, swollen with pollen,
A long halloo, a highpitched howl,
A dog in summer weather, a flag
That luffed and luffed, a boat that disappeared,
A passing sail that turned, that sailed away.

AUTUMNAL

This death is terrible—as if
Some creature lay howling—the animal
That lay outside the window,
And shattered the night. Next morning
You searched for its blood . . . though soon enough
Blood will be everywhere, soaking the leaves,
As at an abattoir (your father told you
Of the pitiful moanings, sticky
On the bloodsmelling air) . . .
This death is terrible—like a train
Looming at the crossroad, and your car
Humped on the tracks, where you see
The headlights nearing
Across the fated, inescapable distance.

What is terrible is to quit the earth
Forever: the air you breathe,
The landscape you love, the woman
You crave as a man craves air, water, light;
The shiver of leaves, the scent of rain,
The memory of heat upon the skin,
As when, as a boy, you dove into water;
The trees a choir of children,
Their voices ringing on the air, and then
Given to flame, given to eating fire.

TOUCH

When you reach out, what do you touch?
And sometimes a hand, and sometimes a peach, and sometimes
Nothing at all. But at the crossroads
It is life you touch, and sometimes
It is lovely, and sometimes
It is terrifying beyond words. But
When you reach—and you must reach,
You have no choice, there is no other turning—
It is always your destiny you touch,
Though it be only a room, a chair,
The sandals you first you put on, running out
Into the morning, how proud you were!
And when you touch, how wonderful!—although
You cannot hear the grasses singing!
For when you touch, you cannot know
You will never touch again, for
The train is leaving (the train
Is always leaving), you wave your hand,
You reach, you touch (it is so close, so lovely!),
You reach to touch the air.

THE LENGTH OF BEING

Stretching to the length of all my being
Stretching to the full extent of being
I see that grass is home and habitation
Other than air, which is a habitation
Of spirit and of spirits like the air
That wander in the thinner realm of air
Raising themselves above our mortal earth
Which is our home, compounded of the earth.
Nothing has changed, we are just what we were
And destined for the earth, just as we were
To give ourselves to earth and lie in grass
And come and disappear just like the grass
Being composed of vanity and fire
Which is an element that can aspire
Unto that other element the air
That freedoms in the wider circumsphere,
Yet is the breathing space of living men
That lifts us upward though we are but men
And lie in earth and know the grass our being
And humbly thank the earth for our small being
Although we disappear and leave the air
To close the empty space where once we were.

WAITING

You return to me, familiar ghost,
You return as a young woman,
In the corridors of memory, there
Where we touch the corner of eternity.
You return, Mother, young woman,
As I knew you, as you were
In that dimension so gone,
So disappeared, like rainfall
Into the sea. You return,
Brown hair, brown eyes, as mortal
As you or I, *Lecteur*, moving in sunlight,
Doing the things a mother used to do
So there could be a center,
An overarching, a holding upright,
A passing through—as the soul
Holds upright against time, space,
Disappearance, going away,
Going under, as a small boy
Falls backward into water
And his mother is beside him instantly—
Or isn't beside him, has disappeared, has
Gone forever, and the water is
Life, your life, whatever we call life,
For you are moving through shadows
In corridors where the familiar ghost
Is moving, is passing, is waiting.

POEM

My three belovèd dead
stand at the edge of the bed
casting a ghostly light
against the dark midnight
which shuts in like a lid
the place where they lie hid.
I see as in a dream
lit by the still eyebeam
my three belovèd dead
living now instead
of crushed where they were caught
by life's cruel Juggernaut.
I see my father stand
and bless me for the while
extending his kind hand
and his remembered smile,
although his death was worse
than any mortal curse.
David my brother there
close beside my bed
stands in the moony glare
that rings the ghostly dead;
David, my lovely brother,
gone like any other
down to bottomless death
although his warming breath
lights upon my cheek
as if from just last week.
Where are the dead, and how

do we remember now,
not by our own intent,
their lovely lineament?
There is my mother, she
who gave life's breath to me,
beloved begetter, love
of my first decades; of
all my days and years;
there is my mother, she
I've loved since infancy,
dead now, in the grave,
unblessed for all she gave.
Father, lovely brother,
Mother—dearest mother!
bless me now, I pray,
take this cup away;
though now this love be broken,
made of dust, of air
that lights our little sphere;
stay beside me, stay,
though not a word be spoken
beside my sleeping bed
where the eternal dead
stand and offer me,
brief though it must be,
love's immortality.

THE THINGS WE SHARED

The things we shared,
Bach on the radio, books
like cardigans, words
we invented, love
we thought we had invented—
California in California sunlight,
Paris in Paris rain . . . your body
"A field of grasses where I played".
Paradise! Fool's paradise!
The idiot notion that
one thing could be right.

It was you who were right . . .
your heart the pump we used—
a sponge wrung out too often,
from the brilliant flash of youth
to the almost indifference of middle age.
It is your heart we celebrate,
the cry of love, the sigh
of exasperation, the insistence
that all things be right;
the one who causes yes
to spring up like flowers;
a lifetime where I held
a single shape, a single name—
the long distance runner who,
still, at midnight, puts
one foot, stubbornly,
in front of the other.

THE LAND OF UNKNOWING

It happened that everything was taken away.

Not only spring; not only
Sunlight along the edge of grass;
But your mother at thirty-five,
Her voice, the color of her hair, so that,
Encountering a forgotten photograph,
You are stopped as by a stranger.

And the woman you loved, the woman
You thought you knew. . . she too
A figment of imagination,
A compound of need and desire,
As if in the ceaseless diminution of being
There was only thirst, only hunger—
An element with the half-life of a day.

ii

So there it stood, the shape of desire,
As if, as if, as if. . .We were walking,
We were holding hands, we crossed
Into another country. The air was the same,
The movement of the leaves—how did we know
It was a different continent, an undiscovered land?
We lay in the grass and sunlight braided your hair.
It was an El Dorado of happiness, a new language,
A space invented by us alone . . .

iii

The circle is always broken,
A flaring up... a dying down...
A guttering out. You
Can no longer know
The path by the meadow,
The flank of the horse,
The voice repeating your name . . .
Look! over your shoulder,
In sunlight, in shade,
The people you loved,
Behind you,
Where light breaks
On brick, on leaf—
The land of unknowing!

iv

Bleed into the gutter!
Bleed! The world lies
Like a man
Thrown from a car,
Sprawled on the pavement.

v

Angel, fly low, touch with mercy
The transience of our being. Be
The voice of love. Be
The woman who loved you.
Become the emanation of
Forgiveness—as the mind

Arises new-made out of sleep,
Refreshed like the day,
Uplifted into the light.

SAYING

Not being able to say
What I always wanted to say,
I consent to the silence that grows
Like a field that's abandoned in rows
Where birds rise flapping in air,
Black sun on their wings, and where
At the end of the field, like a man,
A scarecrow is hung-out to stand.

An inch of fire from here
(Where words are sealed up by lips
Tight closed around teeth, and the tips
Of sunlight burn in the eye
Like thorns as a child goes by)
Suffices to get us to there—
A garden, a pathway, a field,
A way that is newly revealed,
The flip side of all left unsaid—
To say what has to be said.

But though I am longing to know
The steps of that dance, and the grace
To carry me back to that place,
There's a way I know I can't go,
Where words fit to meaning, and meaning
Fits to the contour of seeming
As puns to the playing of wit,
Or body to body will fit.
There meaning is just what we say,

And words are enough to convey
The burden of love, and enough
To say to our love that we love.

WHAT, O WHAT

What, O what,
slipped through your fingers?
What images? The
leap of the cat, the
gallop of the horse, the
sway of
sweet Timothy weed . . .
Who can tongue
the nameless, throat
the ineffable?
What O what
that stung, that bit
that spit? Why
the eye plucked out,
the thin throat cut,
the sharp hiss
serpented? Why
the irrevocable?

Summer
spreads its blanket;
winter
slings it ice;
autumn
smears its blood;
spring
flies off, carrying with it
the girl you loved

transfigured to a flower.

NOTHING HAS CHANGED

Nothing has changed: the barbarians
swarm down from the north, ice
sharpens its knives, plague
tightens the throat. The church
offers dispensation, commits
simony, denounces the Jews.
Uncharitable winter freezes the bone.

It is an illusion
that anything has changed. Man is born,
flesh is threshed like grass. The world
hangs by a thread—by its neck.
Why should anything be different?
You are the sinner, you the son of man.

Let us begin again. Let us shoulder our burden.

FOR KATIA

My darling girl, my daughter,
You who carry hope like water
Through the dessert! Afraid
Of nothing! Not even life!
That brandishes its teeth,
Not like a bear, but like a wolverine,
Which even a bear avoids. My girl!
Grown to a woman! How
I would give you happiness!
Lifting you in my arms as
Long ago—now launched
On the mammoth, rolling,
Unstoppable waves, where
Voyagers travel alone,
Destiny yours to grapple,
Sacred banner that in your hand
You raise, staring into the wind, where, onward,
Darling, with all our love, you go!

FALLING THROUGH EARTH

Falling through earth,
At last you come to the end of the earth.
Everything is the same,
the faces the words the trees—only
you have reached the end of the earth.

This is you, immured
in the cycle of the self,
the stutter of the motor, the ache
of the break of the bone . . .

Falling through earth,
you come at last to the wall
where you must stand,
since not to stand
is to die . . .
                    The meadow
arches its light; the eternal
mouth of the earth
turns upward,
sucking the sun.

PRAYER

Come with me, be be be!—
such the cry of the molecule
to the element; the flame
to the oxygen, the lover
to the beloved, eaten
in sacrament . . . .

What blood spilt on stone,
what genuflection
in the mythology of ignorance?

Ground us now
in the knowable accompaniment,
the voice we hear,
the uncreated creating
creation, the eternal
revelation:
          I will not let thee go
except thou bless me!

BOOK IV

(2010 – 2012)

ON THE TIP OF THE TONGUE

ON THE TIP OF THE TONGUE

It seemed on the tip of the tongue,
The words that you wanted to say—the sentences
That would sum up a lifetime. It
Didn't appear so difficult, as if words
Were adequate, as if the mind were adequate,
As if *your* mind were adequate . . . as if
The heat of summer could be worded,
The rasp of insects, the skitter of wind,
The moisture hanging heavily in the air,
Hanging . . . ready to drop—like words
Heavy and hanging on the tip of the tongue.

THE BRAVE SEAS

The brave seas that have swallowed so many,
The highways, the dead dogs by the highways,
The children singing as they enter
The imaginary heaven of their mothers,
The doom that is dark as any sea dingle
And crouches in closets, in chemicals,
And seeps in our bloodstream like mortality,
The sentence, the hangman, the noose . . . .

I know that the world was made for praising,
As a child for loving, as a woman for loving,
As a young man for suppleness and grace;
And that the sin for which there is no forgiveness
Is the saying nay, the turning away,
The dark that blots the sun, that spots
The traveled highway, the children at their play,
Where women rise at break of day
To stretch, to choose a dress, to touch your hand.

THE WAY

The single way was waiting,
Coded like phlox in the genes,
Like marigolds, which bring in
Laurels and bright weather. But you recall
The tower with its arrow-slits,
With wipes in the corners, with
The odor of urine, the turret
Overpreening the valley,
As hawthorn gives way to peach, and evening
Drops like a stone into ocean.

But the paths were innumerable,
Pointing in all directions, as the motor
Idled under the window.
And you counted on your wrist
The tick of life's blood,
The fortuitous eternal choices
Where you lay you down
In the arms of the mortal princess.
Love was pap and grit
And points of the compass,
As you swung the prow of the ship,
Maneuvering the sand bars.

Wanderer, inquirer, journeyman,
Trust the inconstant current,
Its flowing, snakelike and undulant,
Its monstrous, insouciant power.
Trust the tongue that translates

Chemicals into nourishment;
The inevitable green slime
That eggs becoming; the bluey atmosphere;
The footloose highways—trust
Our home, our dark and faithless home.

WALK OUT AT NIGHT

Walk out beneath the stars,
The congregation of arbitrary inter-
connectedness, like human congress,
The awesome, sidereal Nothing
That even Aristotle, that sober-
minded man, believed divine.

Behold the darksome Otherness
Of Overarching, nocturnal Thereness,
Astrological bewilderment
That the astounding Mayans, the Babylonians,
Computed like arithmetic
And worshipped as theophany.

Be now the blackness that is firstness
In the stillness where you wander,
Where, looking upward, you wonder,
Believing in primal wonder,
Like a wolf, like a man,
Watching in carnal ignorance.

Become the Here of Immediacy
And the Now of Otherness,
The instantaneous foreignness
Of sight, dear as music or leaves; be
That single moment in the blood when,
Unknowable, the innumerable stars prick out.

FOR PETER

Now that the hard metallic sound of intelligence
is dimmed, or dented, or accepted
as the inheritance or the lucky draw
of any preacher's son, and the donné
of just plain being alive out-trumps
any minor accouterment or accomplishment,
as primary qualities were thought to precede
all secondary, the accidents of
color, taste, touch, the wondrous stuff
that makes our world so loveable;
now that across the table we can see
the wrinkles and gray hair of our father,
the skin and underlip of our mother,
I hear you say,

           "My poor brain
can't take in a single thing about it—
its whirling atoms and accidental proficiency,
like the proverbial monkey and the typewriter.
I suppose I still accept some variation
of Lucretius, his democratic atoms
endowed with the inexplicable ability
to swerve, like the smallest amoeba
darting beneath the microscope,
now here now there,
too small for God, too random
for determinism . . . The tales
they tells us nowadays are fairy tales
that make the science fiction of Milton
seem the sanest fabulation: big bangs, cosmic strings,

parallel universes, like those boxes
stacked within boxes, and at the center
nothing at all. Spilled poetry
concocted by poetasters trope-happy with
the heady language of metaphor . . .
what I do each day as Quixotic as
the outgrown inheritance
of a misplaced ideology whose asseverations
I no longer bother to read . . . I regret,
O, so many things! My heady youth
chock-a-block with anger and contempt,
a wicker basket where I stuffed
my dirty laundry. . . ."

          —Speaking for myself,
this much I've never regretted:
loving you. . . loving everyone
I've ever loved, mother, father, wife,
the random assortment of life
that mounts and floats away.
Not-understanding is itself
a philosophy, the large-tomed encyclopedia
of our ignorance, decked out
with all the medals and citations we won
in high school, those faux-gold plaques
our father saved, then finally
threw away. I am content
to play Aeneas to your Prometheus—
pious Aeneas, who carried his father
on his own back; the two of us
two peas from a pod, two destinies

tied by love and heritage—two
brothers united as closely
as love and consanguinity can knot.

THE STRANGER MUST DIE

To say it didn't turn out
as you expected, is to say
the least of it. . . . To move at all
is error, although
moving is the very condition
of life . . . .

You cannot recognize the shape of your life
until it returns, loops back again,
recurring in sudden recognition, so that
you acknowledge the familiar error.

To say you expected otherwise
is to confess your ignorance,
a darkness, a mystery—like Oedipus,
who never admitted he was guilty.

At the turning of the crossroads,
you meet your face in the face of the approaching stranger,
arrogant, demanding precedence;
but when you strike,

the knife will strike to the heart,
everything shall be permitted,
wife mother children;
you have struck yourself

through the heart,
and the stranger must die.

TO SPEAK ONE'S NAME

Stopped! stopped by love,
that cannot speak its name!—

As in August, when mid-summer
lies in its weeds. I would convey

what is unsayable, a small mountain
humped in midnight,

a clot of darkness, light
on the branches of winter . . .

So many things call out
for love, summer in its fragrance,

birdsong at morning, bats
in their sharp-winged flight . . . yes!

you tried . . . you tried to say . . .
but were stopped, were stopped by love,

that cannot speak its name!

FOR NATHAN, FIVE YEARS OLD

My elf, my little angel, my grandson!
You who charge with life a word like *angel*;
Whose visage stops the casual passing stranger
With wonder at forgotten innocence.

As a pool of water catches the light
Within the shimmering border of its arms,
In which the curious fish, like your small thoughts,
Flash their fins in silver-colored flight;

Like flaming quartz, like a twirling feather;
So you, my prancer, my small miracle,
Teach again the wonder of becoming,
A lesson lost—then suddenly remembered.

Love is the meaning of our life, dear child,
And flashes like a diver in his fall,
Filling with joy the daring of becoming,
Like breath with love at merest sight of you.

HOW IT ENDS

It always ends with a wall,
a bed against a wall,
white sheets and the blankness of a wall.

It ends with blood for the soldier,
terror for the child,
filling the room like ammonia.

There is no escaping
the error, the indictment
like a shadow in an empty sleeve.

It always ends in a cry
that rises and rises—
and fills the universe.

LOVE'S PROFIT

What is your touchstone for love if not
That dazzling girl, now long since dead?
Everyone warned you against her,
"*La belle dame sans merci*," they said.
And you? A nincompoop, of course,
Wet behind the ears, eager as a balloon
To pop. Who can count love's profit?
An incomprehensible jibberish, like
Sentences in demotic French. Forty years!
(Though you recall in perfect kinesthesia
Her calves, smooth as sea-glass.)
What was she up to, that sixteen year old
In a movie by Antonioni, drifting
Through the treacherous shoals of adolescence?
Well, that was in another country, and besides,
The wench is dead—although you've been married to her now
For forty years! . . . What your touchstone
If not that girl, love's loss, love's profit,
Slipping down memory like a billet-doux,
A beauty now of sixty with gray in her hair,
The idol of your life, *Ma femme fatale! Ma femme!*

FIRST DAYS

In the long first days of love,
when, after love, there was always
more love; in that season of young love
when love was Meaning, the summa bonum;
in that fierce flush, when you lay
like a sloop beside me, with passion
of sudden waves—what profit
in that arithmetic of loving, of tallying,
of divvying up; that El Dorado
that gets shared out like dog food? . . .

               And yet, and yet . . .
there is always love, although it lie
deep seeded beneath the actual,
the incontinent continuing mystery
which simmers like summer;
the inexhaustible rain
that dews the earth, hovering
in impenetrable cloud, then rising
in mist to fall again. And so
the seasons turn round in a climate
where even winter
offers promise of perennial miracle.

SONG

Why are the sparks of light in song,
Bursting in sound in ruby red?
If you could say, would you ever say
Why the sparks of light are in song?

Why do the leaves, the leaves of the air
Dip their tallits everywhere?
If you dipped a cup in the rushing stream
The tallits of water would burst into song.

The sun was in song and the sunsong said
Praise the sparks of the living dead,
Dip your cup in the livelong stream,
Drink the sunlit sparks of song.

HOLD MY HAND

Dearest friend, dearest friend in the wilderness,
The past is a shawl, though the wind blows through it.

The wind, the wind! It tears the tops of the trees.
Memories rain down like branches!

Look! . . . The air is where we drown! Down! Down!
Where bottom? Where the extended believable oxygen?

Where the heaven with shining transparent Overness?
The awaited cottage, the winding path?

Come with me! Come! We will never be parted!
Hold my hand in the wilderness, dearest friend.

A GARDEN, A PATIO

In this woman you can see
A garden, a patio, a tree,
A graceful sway, a way to be
In complex simplicity,
Like water running in its course,
Like music dancing in discourse,
Daily weaving life in one
Gathered, intertwining sum,
A garden, and the gardener's art
To plant a garden in the heart,
To set a life in beds and rows
Until the budded green plant grows
Like her own herbaceous mind,
Into the grace of womankind.
In this woman you behold
Riches in simplest manifold,
No fairy tale, mythology,
But apples from the golden tree!

JEOPARDY

Love was always in jeopardy,
the perilous slope, the precipitous descent,
the breakneck landing.
If I should list the ways
of failure, the I-ness, the darkness,
the blindness of sunlight, the rock-
unstopableness of earth . . . words
spoken in anger, words
spoken in pettiness, words
spat against the wall. Who knows this
better than I? Sinbad
circling the terraqueous globe
with handspan life-raft,
with incontinent compass,
with leaky, unusable pail . . . .

IF SHE STANDS BEFORE YOU

If she stands before you sheathed in light,
It is because the grace of early womanhood
Touched her with its peculiar splendor; and
If she stands before you sheathed in light,
It is because the moment of adolescence
Lit her with its incandescence; and
Where she lay her down in the first fierce sunburst of love,
What was she but the heart-pulse of pleasure? and
When her breasts bequeathed a stream of light,
What was she but the incarnation of motherhood?
And the lines that are etched now on her brow
Like the fine cracks in chalcedony porcelain—
What of these? For if she stands before you sheathed in light,
It is because she was always the one at the end of the path
Waiting for you in sunlight, waiting in a passion of sunlight,
Waiting for you in a passion of light.

THE TRUEST POEMS

I think of the poems that fell between the cracks,
Were never completed, were only partially completed,
The truest poems, the ones that caught most truly
Our broken condition, our uncompleted act.
For everything is broken, though not in parts
That fit together—that would be too easy.
The words are all a-jumble, here *Hand,*
Here *Heart,* here *Home*—as in a game,
And we the players, we the speaking-ones,
Who mound the heaps of Thereness like a child
Puzzling out his maps, piling his sand . . . .

Be now the poem of air, the brilliant ballerina,
The imperfect perishable in the arc of perfection,
As on the highway you see the heat-waves rising.
Be the silence that fits inadequate speaking,
The sentence, the unknown syllable—be
The countless words that fell from midnight's table.

TRANSLATIONS

(The following translations are "imitations",
as in Pope, or Lowell's volume of that title.)

TO ANACTORIA

Some think the most beautiful thing
is soldiers falling into line; some think,
warships riding at sea.

Nothing is as beautiful as my love.

I can easily make you understand this. For

didn't Helen, the belle of all, fall
for the lowest scoundrel, the scum
of Troy, deserting child, husband? . . .

Women are like that, bestowing
too much love, now here,
now there—wherever Love may fall.

On this dark earth, I know,
we cannot keep the best—the flash
of your bright face!—but

remember, Anactoria! parted forever,
whose slightest footfall
outshone the tempered steel! for

once to have known you
is never to forget!

—Sappho (612 bce– ?)

I am by now so wearied of this waiting

I am by now so wearied by this waiting,
So beaten by this sadness and desire,
Because of the faithlessness, because of the forgetfulness
Of him I love, who, far away, distains
His promise to return, that I cry out
To Her, who with her sickle makes the world
Pale as grief, white as grass—whose punishment
Yet stirs more deeply in my woman's heart
This endless pain. But She is deaf to me,
Disdainful of the folly of my thoughts,
As he to any thought of his return,
So that my eyes make swim with useless tears—
With stinging tears—these waves, this pitiless sea,
While he, happy in far off hills, stays far away.

—Gaspara Stampa (c. 1523 – 1554)

Kennst du das Land?

Knowest thou the land where the lemon trees bloom?
In darkling leaves the golden blossoms bloom.
A scented wind keeps blowing through the air,
The myrtles sleep, the bay leaves brush the air.
Knowest thou such place?—O there, O there!
O, my beloved, that I could take you there!

Knowest thou the house? On columns rests the roof.
The sun is shining from the polished roof.
The marble statues stand and stare at me;
What has the world (they ask me) done to thee?
Knowest thou such place?—O there, O there!
O, my master, could you but take me there!

Knowest thou the cloudy mountain path?
Through mists the mule must thread its dangerous path.
Within its den the dragon guards her brood,
Down the deep cliff the fast streams fall in flood.
Knowest thou these things?—O there, O there
Our true path runs . . . O Father, lead us there!

—Johann Wolfgang Goethe (1749 – 1832)

TO HIMSELF

Now rest forever, my heart!
that final deception is dead,
I know it well! depart-
ed, that lovely deception,
not only the hope, but even
the desire is dead! That commotion
of yours is not worth
a penny—don't bother your head!
the earth is not worth
a penny. Bitter and noisome—
the world is mud.
Be silent!
and for the last time
despair. Death
is our only gift. Dismiss
forever that brute thing,
Nature, that rules the universe; dismiss
the utter vanity of everything.

—Giacomo Leopardi (1798 – 1837)

THE JEWELS

The belovèd was naked and, knowing my desire,
She had left on nothing but her sonorous jewels,
Which lent her nakedness, as to a Moorish slave,
The harem beauty of their flickering fire.

When dancing it lets flash its mocking sound,
This world of glowing metal and of stone
Ravishes to ecstasy—to madness I adore
This swooning source that sound and sense compound.

Thus she lay, giving herself to love,
Smiling from the height of her divan
At my deep passion, rising strong and high
As a high rip-tide mounts into a cove.

Her eyes were fixed upon me like the eyes
Of a young tigress, leashed and in repose,
Whose languid hunger lends lubricity
The constant shifting candor of surprise.

Her arms, her polished legs, the perfect line
That fell from neck to thigh, the up-turned breasts,
Polished like oil, undulant as the swan's,
Offered up the firm grapes of the vine.

These she swagged before me, corrupt child!
Angel of evil, born to hurl my soul
Down from its haven in its crystal tower
To her ripe flesh, by which my heart's beguiled.

I saw united as by a new design
The hips of Antiope with the bust of a boy—
So much her figure favored my own style!
And on the skin the soft cosmetic shine!

But now the lamp resigns itself to death.
Only the guttering fire illumes the bed.
Each sigh of flame ignites her tawny flesh,
Flushed with the pulse of her flint-hearted breast.

—Charles Baudelaire (1821 – 1867)

World Was in the Face of the belovèd

World was in the face of the belovèd.
But then it fled–quite suddenly it fled!
World was outside—out of my possession!

Why, when once I could, did I not drink
Out of the then, out of the well loved face,
World, so close, so welcome to my lips?

Ah, I drank! Unstoppably I drank!
But I was also filled with too much World,
And, drinking deeply, overflowed the cup.

—Rainer Maria Rilke (1875 – 1926)

Let absence be always behind you

Let absence be always behind you,
like winter, that's already fled;
for under winter there lies—O, such another winter!
that, overwintering, your heart must surely bestead.

Be always dead in Eurydice! Out-singing, arise!
out-praising, sing back to the pure relation!
Here, in the realm of decline,
sing like a glass that rings in its breaking!

Be! And be mindful of our own Unbeing,
the unceasing ground of our one only being,
that this, your one time, you may fill with singing!

To the used, the mute, the forever silent—
the uncountable storehouse of bottomless being—
count joyfully out, and square the account!

—Rainer Maria Rilke (1875-1926)

RESURRECTION OF LOVE IN THE
RECURRENCE OF LIVING LANDSCAPE

Believe, my love, as I do, that the landscapes
we loved, remain asleep
or dead within us, in that very hour, that instant
in which we knew them; and the trees
give up their memory, and the nights
trail on, relinquishing to forgetfulness
those things that made them lovely
or even immortal, perhaps;

until that moment of the slightest breeze—
the single shudder of a star—which is enough
to wake, to make again
the happy lovers that we were, who still contain
the landscape that contained us once.

Here are still the dewy rocks, the chips
of wood that perfumed then your bed,
the dream-sylphs that decked your hair in dreams,
and the elusive squirrels that rained your sleep
with smallest twigs of green.

Be happy, happy leaf, nor ever know
the winds of autumn; you who with your slightest quiver
carried the odor of those luminous days;
and you, small star, that opened
the intimate windows of departed youth—
never extinguish your light that shines
on alcoves where the dawn alone brought sleep,

nor on those moonlit books of fluttering leaves,
nor mountains with their far, persistent song.

—Rafael Alberti (1902 - 1999)

HALF A TURN

HALF A TURN

With a half a turn you might call it sinister,
Birds yanking worms from the grass,
Ice pouring down like Vikings,
Slaughtering leaves, snakes eating flies,
Flies biting children—a carnival
Of death, as in the cinema—
Here and here and everywhere . . . like beauty!

Although perhaps it is a form of stupidity
To see it as beauty and not death—to see
The infinite profusion of green
As beneficence, a joy to the eye,
An energy, the forming Energy,
Being instead of Nothing, the firefly
But not the devouring flame.

Now, beneath the canopy of leaves,
Beneath the trees, the air
Is Possibility, the accession of breath,
The unlikely coming into being
Of us, the grace of the Divine,
Since not to call it divine
Is dumbness, is stupidity, is deaf.

TIME MACHINE

This flesh at my middle—this middle age,
What is it but the loosened knot
Of youth, my salad days—the age
That gripped me in my flesh-proud spring,
And blinded and exalted and betrayed?
Now the spiky sky-blue transcendence
Pierces to heaven, and what is known
Remains untellable. O life, O simple life,
Your bounty exceeds expression, conferring
A sacrament of praise. Duck and flower
Squawk with the fatty tissue of living,
And being sticks like tar to the hands.
Release like alcohol the serotonin
Of felicity; breathe for the dead
The Now of Here, which is theirs
No longer—and yours
By gift and grace alone; the ongoing
Illusion, as once upon a time
The incarnation of love from salt and blood,
The unrepeatable eternity of mortality,
The bending down, the kissing, the disappearing.

TIME AND IMAGINATION

It happened that time fell on him
And crushed him to the ground.
And there like a worm he crawled,
He struggled. And the weight
Equaled the weight of being alive, piled
Like a circus act on his shoulders.
This was death, certainly at some point
This would be dying, as the ant
Beneath the heel, the man
Beneath the avalanche . . . What is time
But the medium of alienation, so that
We see each object, each hour, taken away,
As a child his favorite toys?

But as we grow older the real
Becomes a permanence, or at least
The site of such permanence, so that
The flowing becomes a remembering,
And this within-ness provides
A point of purchase, a comparison
To judge (though not to stop) the passing.
Life, the only one we've known, inflicts
The wounds that kill, as in the hunt
The arrows in the lion's side. Or in
The tapestry, where the unicorn,
Dying, is hounded by dogs
And men—but rests in the lap of the lady
The shape of mercy, the dreamt-of Princess,

The mother, the wife, the remembered—
The Un-time stolen from time, the woof
Wherein she aids, she breathes, she comforts,
In the heraldic garden where she waits.

PRAISE

What this floodgate, this waterspout
As in a garden the upsoaring fountain?
Is it not the act of praise, the
Unexcelled, the incommensurate?
Here, now, confess the uselessness
Of all but praising, since virtue
Is unattainable; confess
The somatic health of thankfulness,
Since body and soul are one,
A mystery, the inextricable oneness
Of the I—and praise is health. This
The primary commandment,
Spontaneous as vanilla, difficult as chess,
The welling up of gratitude
As a man breathes sunlight,
Loves a child, strokes an animal,
Sings in the morning, opens a window,
Inhales the air, praises the light,
Loves the recurrent energy of being alive.

EDENLAND

I am talking about a cottage, a summer day,
An afternoon of Latin, your faithful companion
There beside you; your parents, your brothers;
The music of Bach, the music of Palestrina;
Love in the afternoon, knowing that love
Is paradise (as I've said before), a glimpse
Of Paradise—who says we can't return?
Although it's only life lived over again,
Eternal life! . . . I'm speaking now
Of what should be: love, friendship, music,
A cottage by a river—the waters of life
Coursing through Edenland, our ancient home,
Our dreamt of destination, Godhead
Like sunlight everywhere! Our heritage, our inheritance!

ROBIN SONG

Red robin, bright robin, swift friend,
Where do you go at summer's end?
With buttercup, with dandelion, with grass,
Days that through the sunlight pass,
Diamond days, jewels on grassy ways
As sunlight through the shadowed branches plays,
Melon-light, light of peach and apple,
Lights that on the moving meadows dapple
The silver seeming, sliding, swift-voiced stream
That calls to us, that laughs with its bright beam,
Whose language is the drifting sunny hour
Dissolving in the raindrops, whose swift shower
Showers hill and leaf and blade of grass
With shining eardrops, quick and liquid as
A blade of light, the light of passing May,
The rosy robin's note at quick of day,
Which disappears, which flees with summer's end—
Red robin, bright robin, briefest friend.

THE BEAUTIFUL GARDEN

Here stands the house and here the beautiful garden
Of English poetry, part in words,
And part in shining air, like a diver
Flashing through distance. Here
The lexicon of living, like a deck of cards. Here
The rose and here the oxeyed daisy
And here the row of gilly flowers,
Like glisters all of syllables, like a man
Made all of air, a storm of weather.
Here the beautiful establishment
Of English verse—a singing symphony,
A spot in summer, a sunny spot,
A place in which we pause and freely breathe.

THE MOUNTAINS OF THE MIND

In the mountains of the mind there stands
A place called No-Belief: here the valleys,
Here the villages, here the fields—
The dim gray space of everyday. Here
Small man lives in comfort, larger man
In discontent, for all is grounded here
In earth, in mud, compounded
With death. No-Belief is decked
With illusion: the clouds are barbe
De papa, the days a daisy chain.
Immortality is just another name for *Here*,
(Grandma waves from heaven, calling
Too-da-loo!), while round about
The walls of the mind, the unmovable,
The adamantine cliffs of Not-Beyond.
Above in sunset grandeur the high peaks
Of Far-Above, hooded in ice.
One crosses one crosses one crosses
The valley of No-Belief, one breathes
Its vapid air, it is our home. For here
All is placebo: science, money, sex—
The mumbo-jumbo of human endeavor.
But ah! that mountain freedom
Ledged and climbing; seeing
As the falcon sees, with fifty times our sight,
The thinning air, the gathering cold,
The fateful parting of the mountain clouds!

ON 53rd STREET

On 53rd Street, in a ventricle of my city,
On the 23rd floor of a polished sky-scraper,
Far above the clash of secular traffic
In the dispensation of Late Capitalism,
I saw, as I exited my well-appointed office—
Cubicle and sanctuary of profane imagination—
There, beyond the glass to the elevator,
The Japanese cleaning man, the color of faded tobacco,
Bowing, Japanese-fashion, from the waist
(Believing himself unseen) before
The honored, the elegant, the alien ficus tree.

CITY

Out of the beckoning, careening, bright-light city
You look to discover
Flags clouds planes bridges towers
Choices and the opportunity for more choices
As at a steeple race, a carnival,
Or the vast intricate contradictory continent of philosophy.

Why are there not more voices to declare
Here is the ultimate place, the destination!
With its onyx, its chrysoprase
Like tongue-twisters in an inflected language,
Its cotton candy, its chestnuts
Its young people with eager unlikely hypotheses.

Praise brick stone glass steel
Architecture crowds of different faces
Races beautiful unexpected features
Unexpected expenditures in restaurants
Sweetbreads, olives, expensive Chianti,
For marriages pleasures unending significant adventures.

This the place, the celebration,
As legs and shoulders jostle for exits
And daylight yawns at vaulting distance
And meanings compound their multiple possibility
On high heels, on the West Side Highway
In the cavorting astounding unstopable metropole.

ILSFORD

Ilsford, Isle of colored stones,
Isle of roundbacked combes, of sluicing streams,
Isle of clouds, Isle of shadows,
Isle of sweetsmelling parsley
In dells, in declivities where dimpled sheep
Baa and sleep like lumpy sweaters,
Isle where swains upon their self-made pipes
Serenade Clarissa with their pastorals,
O Ilsford, O unfound periphery;
Cloudy and sacramental as a dream,
Stuck in a corner like a postage stamp,
Discovered in books, in encyclopedias,
Decked out in grass, in Timothy weed,
Like a lassie in a hayfield;
O pastoral imagination, ivory someplace,
Junket of playfulness and fond beauty,
Like to a girl of fifteen, like to a song,
Like to a tale that's told by an idiot
For the sake of telling, the poet's hideaway,
The poet's insight, the poet's privilege,
Place of fancy and freefold imagination,
O Ilsford, Isle of colored stones.

FOR ASHER

Asher
Dear Other
In sweetest
Proportion
Our smallest
Our newest
From Ocean
From Mother
O, Greetings!
You loved one
My earthling
My precious
So lovely
Dear breather
Dear heartbeat
My bloodline
My loveline
Who loves you
Forever
You tiny
Wee package
With all love
For all time
O, Other
O, Asher
Our darling
Our boy!

LINES FOR SIMONE

Simone, my darling, my next to daughter,
everything disappears, of you your infancy,
of others their love. Too early, this,
for little ears, Simone, my pipsqueak,
my immortality. Like your mother,
you grace our bones with gracefulness,
like a balalaika, a ballerina,
you sonata in a language of genetics,
you salad from a summer garden.
Grace now with your dear blood, Simone,
the heartblood of my bleeding,
as I would grace my daughter,
who stood above beyond below
the need of my own heartstring, of my heart.

MY BODY MY ENEMY

My body, my enemy,
Dumb mechanism, clogged obscurantist,
Cloak of otherness, doughy selfhood,
This gibberish, this oration,
This hillock where we're hanged, this nexus of necessity,
This pain forestalled, this mounting decrepitude—
Old buddy, old tinker, old fleshpot,
How long since you have thickened like soup
From that once lad, that airy plaything,
That floater on windfree, that boyhood—
O enemy-mine, o me!

My friend, my body,
Who soaks like mud in sunlight
Who sniffs, who swaggers
Who feels along his arms his nerve-ends,
The tickle of sweetest windpipe, of fair song,
Who swallows like cider the Other,
The sight of sweetness, the site,
The thick of companionship, the weft
Of seeing hearing touching tasting
Earth and world and lovely matter,
Fat champion, redoubtable dunce
O jester o playmate o princeling,
Quotidian companion, certain death.

SPIRITUAL REALITY

Spiritual reality is always incarnate,
Knows the melancholy of the body,
Rides the trajectory of the body;
Like a stone, like a human,
Obeys the inexorable force of gravity
Knows itself, delights itself
Celebrates the kindful act of being
Like a flower faced toward sunlight.
This the fact, spiritual, unchangeable,
Manifest to every mother's child,
Though pride would have it otherwise:
A machine, a self-running gadget,
A perpetuum mobile, an impossibility—
Not the single, incarnate spirit
That fell into being, that awaits revelation
Like mind behind the tight skullpan,
Like eye that stretches sight to vision.

SHORTS

i

Love is that stuff that's given all in all,
Or if not so, best given not at all.

Not so! Love speaks its chosen part,
But leaves some things recusant in the heart.

ii

Split down the middle, as we are,
Bleeding still beneath the scar,
Men and women, to be true,
Must form a oneness out of two.

iii

Da-da-da cries the baby,
And maybe—just *maybe*,
By the time she calls you Father,
She'll still seem worth the pain and bother.

iv

Words the spirit goes through
Are fashioned like bamboo
To let the spirit rise
Or sink down otherwise
So that the spirit can
Go downward or expand
Growing as we grow
Beyond the things we know

And thus with quick surmise
Surprise us with surprise!

v

Concerning my friends the birds
I know no other words
To greet our summer guests
Except what's said in jest.
For birds are not inclined
To words of human kind,
Which must supply the source
Of human intercourse;
But those of a feathered nature
Shun our nomenclature
And use a different fare,
Skimming the light air.
They find that quite enough
To keep them safe above
Mankind's loquacity,
To which they pipingly
Answer as they will,
Now sweeter, now more shrill,
In ascending thirds,
Instead of human words.

vi

What I wanted to say
gets repeated,
like words
that start at the center,
and circle the center,

to end
where they began, but
at the circumference.

THE ACT OF LOVE

The act of love that brought you into the world,
The free act of love, is woven into the fabric
Of all being and time and is irrevocable,
And exists in the wide unthinkable expanse of the actual
Like a whisper in the farthest aetherium.
What is is indestructible in the backward essentiality
Of being, and cannot be removed or changed,
And lives forever in the imperium of thought
As the smallest fish in the scales of deepest ocean.
This is law and actuality and Mind,
In which the slightest sparrow cannot fall,
A fearsome thought for peccant human kind,
So stuffed with sin, so rife with selfishness,
Yet lit like stars with points of passing grace
That light the night and entertain the day,
The fact that brought you here, the act of love.

FOR MY GRANDCHILDREN

As you grow up, my darlings, as you grow,
You become the various things you know,
You become the various things you love
As we become the things we're compound of.

Backward, Time, like a speeding car,
Disappears in trackless spaces, far
Beyond the power of our poor eyes to see,
Like stones that drop into the depthless sea.

Mother and father, those who gave you life,
Who joined together once as man and wife,
Become again the strangers that they were
Before such consummation could occur.

Flowers that once you cherished, violets
Which your mother taught you, who forgets
In deepest slumber even the bending rose,
Remain forever where the child goes.

Night, that then enclosed you like an eye,
Still burns with insight, like the firefly
Whose momentary flicker you would see
Beneath night's vast emblazed concavity.

World, on which you stand, that lends you strength,
Winds before you in uncounted length

Like a spool of thread, that in array
Hangs the stars in infinite display.

Lift your eyes, lift your sight to see
The bold, unnumbered, strange anatomy
Of being, of unfolding, of love,
Of which no man or woman gets enough.

OFFERING

Today is Easter, and upon this day
I set my mind to offer up a prayer
In teeth of evidence that when we pray
We are the only hearer, we, the only sayer.

I set my mind, I say, to offer up
Memorial to what I don't believe,
Blood and wafer and the mythic cup
Brimful with longed for the make-believe.

But in a different fashion, because once
We woke to celebration with our mother
On Easter morning, with a different sense
Of resurrection, I and my dear brothers;

Children then of course, who now are old,
Yes, almost ancient! and must find a way
To celebrate a story that was told
And now is lost as sure as that first day,

On that strange morning, when young Mary found
The Master risen, and in great surprise,
"Rabbi!" she uttered, seeing face and wound
Before her, to the amazement of her eyes,

As if we saw our mother, who is gone
Into the backward and abysm of lost time,
And cannot come again, however long,
To graced us with her smile at Easter time.

ONCE

Now in the green fields of lyingdown
A lamb is lying in the green field.
Amid the fields, amid the waving grass,
Her tongue is licking the luxuriant grass
As a child the sweet flesh of the apple.

This is to be told at evening by the bed
As the child lies in bed at storytime;
His mother bends above at eventide,
While snug in bed the sleepy child lies
At lyingdown, at evening, with his mother.

LEAVES LIKE OCEANS

Leaves like oceans of light
Fill the eye with eyesight
Praise like song in motion
Moves the heart with its devotion

Ear that can overhear
The swirl of the whirling year—
Such moments of vision
Heal the heart's division

Tongue and ear and eye
Multiply and tie
Strand to parted strand
That would divide the land.

LIFE

The nature of life is such,
Best not to expect too much;
Those who know it best
Think it well expressed
In numbers les than ten
Out of twenty, when
Nodding at the gods,
They tote up the true odds.
Those who think they're winning
Usually end by sinning,
Tripped by their own itch
Into a muddy ditch;
While the humble heart
Watches the Juggernaut
Approaching down the road
To squash him like a toad.

HAUTE CUISINE

If I compared you to a five-star meal,
would that be so ridiculous? For Levi-Straus asserts
that eating is a universal metaphor for sex.
The differences, of course, are obvious:
one can't be gobbled up so quickly! Still,
wine and bread and something French that tastes
delicious? Nor shall I overlook dessert!
I might compare you to the air I breathe,
the earth I stand upon, but just for fun,
and since we were young together in Paris,
I will compare you to a five-star meal!

IN THE STREETS OF MANHATTAN

Days when you wandered through the streets of Manhattan
Dizzy with a young man's existential desire—
Why do you return to me now?
Divided weight pressed forward by gravity
Like the prow of a ship through ocean,
What ocean constricted you with a weight
Heavy as asthma? Baffled, foiled, confused—
What carved your heart like the blade of an Aztec?
This was hunger, this was desire, as the mind
Cries out for the love of a woman, the love
Of *you*, as the partial man
Loves God through His partial creatures,
Fragments of flesh, figures of earth, figments of the love
That rules the sun and the other stars, the love
That dogged me through the streets of Manhattan.

STARTING OVER

In your dream you are in the bottommost office
surrounded by similar offices, a warren
of similar offices; young people
busy with other people's business; your presence
an un-event of the largest dimension.
Outside the window, within an adjacent building,
the World!—the movie studio of the world:
sets, adventures, pornography; around you,
excitement about Richard Gere—the young Richard Gere!—who
(it appears) had worked here once himself; so cool,
so off-beat, so with-it; and you
so un-with-it, so indifferent about
the young Richard Gere . . . Starting over?

You have worked here before—these offices
stretching across the length of this plate-glass building,
these people, these faces, now utterly indifferent,
once so uniformly jubilant, the cheering audience
at a new prime-time tv show; you walk through the offices
alone, the only new kid at a high school,
the corridors unfriendly, the girls untouchable, the kids
a hostile sea of platitude. Starting over?
with the heavy stone of your life
hung like a dog-tag at your neck.

You mayn't enter the last suite of offices. You see
through the plate glass doors that separate you
Angelina surrounded by notoriety, like a princess
by the glitter of decapitation. O Beauty!

O voices with the sweet sound of money
where youth once lost itself in the glossy honeysuckle
of moral exposure. Celebrity swept through you
like influenza. The toad Nostalgia
squats now on your heart; the moon
rises above this squamous scene
like smog over New Jersey. O Now! O
forever-departed Then! What face-lift
could restore the lost promise of ambitious youth
squandered like an exorbitant tip at a bar? And this
the novel you now could write! This, it seems,
the only Then!

THE FLAME

You returned
to the odor of dinner, she
(twenty-nine!)
in the kitchen,
Ariadne with the breasts
of Helen! your daughter
running to greet you
(Daddy! Daddy!)
Purcell on the radio,
Paris outside the window. . . Why, now,
is that happiness?

All things gather—
for what?
(for what (asked Augustine)
is time? that all things
gather
        that all things
fall
     that all things
burn?)

If a man
hang by his arms,
the butterfly wings of his back
will tear,
he will swing
in an ecstasy of agony,
himself

hell . . .

if you love a woman, you
will hang her upside down,
howl, dance
keep others at distance,
break bones
eat flesh
and apologize
never at all . . .

a river
a field of light
which
for an instant
lifts you,
will not
for an instant
release you,
reveals
for an instant
a handkerchief expanse
of sky
a girl
a flower
a flame . . .

the world
is aflame
(says Buddha)
not wisdom but

thunder
the puling
blunder
repeated
over and over
the fire
the child
the wonder
running to greet you
crying

   Daddy! Daddy!

TEARS TEARS TEARS

Tears tears tears
As when a ship disappears
Beneath the deep salt wave
Down to a trackless grave.

So the great Tennyson said,
Speaking no doubt of the dead
Lad, his mate, his dear boy
Who changed long grief to brief joy.

Not idle but deep centered tears
Are what my drowned heart fears,
Filling the dark inner sea
With grief, pain, misery.

Tears tears tears
For the waste of those once happy years
Where a child happily played,
Now lost, destroyed, betrayed.

CURE

Titmouse, Tigger-tail, thyme
Words from a childhood rhyme
As if the world had come
Mediated by love.

Consider the horses once there
In the old Horse Pasture, where
We'd go for picnics, we four,
Who now will picnic no more.

Who now remembers that once
The Pasture stood, which long since
Has turned into white-bricks, where
High-rises crowd out the air?

Consider the things that endure
And those that never recur,
The Pasture where horses once grazed,
Filling small thoughts with long praise.

Walk to the end of the block,
Let sunshine fall on your back,
Let sunlight slowly console
The lost, distempered soul.

TURN AWAY YOUR HEAD

Turn, turn your head
From the grave weight of seeing,
For the dead stand all about you,
Their weight too heavy for seeing.

The earth is feldspar and sun
That flash, that burn the eye;
Tongue cannot taste nor tell
The weight that divides all seeing.

Like the dead in procession,
Still water in a well,
Swimmers foundering in ocean,
Hands that wave farewell;

Like words stuttered in guttural,
Like sentences in free-fall,
The kingdom of Unbeing,
The land of our unseeing.

LAW

Since the world's mountain-dump of That-which-is
remains in me no mountain but a sea,
a sea of ignorance, no wonder should it be
that I go sailing through it; for misprise
of spirit in such tractless, stormy welter,
is taste is touch is will is fallen knowledge,
is learning in the world's great public college
where we matriculate, as if to shelter
against raw appetite, to feed our maw
with fact, with facts, with piled up debris,
with petrafacted lava, with dumb scree,
as if such piled-up artifacts were Law;
so that I turn to right to left, from center,
and miss the door mere facts can never enter.

LINES

Wrap me, wrap me now
in the sodden, exultant air of the present,
wrap me in the mistaken, quotidian contradiction
of hereness, the mortal presence of
thighbone and quince. This is the place for touching,
as the fawn you found in the briars.
And you knelt to release her one by one,
as one unknits the burs from a child's sweater,
till she could stand, not looking back, and walk away.
Wrap me in the shroud of my dailyness,
dizzy with the misapprehension of breathing.
What home what house what door . . . what corridor
where dark light blazes like charcoal,
and the only goal is straw-step? Bright robin,
bright reaper, wrap me now in my daily death,
my enemy, where love leans down like darkness
and blows on the living coal.

PHOTOGRAPHS

Love is these photographs,
the stunning adolescent
playing too well the femme fatale;
the bride anorexic with the anxiety
of new womanhood; the young mother,
herself as beautiful as
the daughters she conjured;
the middle aged success, with her
middle aged crack-up behind her
like a faithful dog: all
incarnations of the woman
I loved and cherished and failed.

We use up the heart,
a piece of chalk, a ballpoint pen,
a cake of Chinese ink left out in the rain . . .
Wanting too much, often we get
too little . . . That muscle,
with its in and out, its in and out,
a bellows, a child's seesaw,
a small boat rocking in waves . . .

The memory returns of a girl
standing in light standing in shadow standing
in life, a girl you can never touch
and never know, whose hand
you held innumerable times,
whose body you held
innumerable times, whose life you shared

your one and only time, your
only journey, your only love.

CONTINUATION

Sing now the singsong of breathing
As the fly the bee the mosquito,
Sing the song of the granddaughter,
Whose skin is smooth as the pie crust
Your mother rolled. That was long ago,
And no one then could know
The granddaughter hiding in the conjunction,
Like the Hudson in the Adirondacks.
Sing the odor of onion grass and skunk cabbage
Swelling beneath the building where you lived,
Heavy as sewage on the midnight air.
Count the generations on your fingers,
Mother daughter grandchild, as the hen
The harried chicks in her inadequacy.
For waves move up and down only,
As one raises one's head in a meadow;
And lark and robin and crow
Are echoes in the inner ear—
As the beautiful child echoes in her cells
The cry the call the continuation.

HOW OFTEN?

How often have I said, I love you?
In how many ways? For how many days,
in hard times and at ease,
when just a boy till now, when death
ticks like a clock on the mantle?
How many gestures, how many words
plucked and arranged like flowers?
what blouse or dress—or undress,
which fit you like a goddess?
How many mountains behind us
like Chinese scrolls? Like a man
who climbs a hill to see
across the landscape to the sea,
which shines before him like a Dufy... This I know,
who know all manner of darkness, where the mind
is hacked with an axe, and midnight
crawls on all fours, and the hand
proffers a stone; this I have known,
who know all portion of splendor—who loved
the way you built our days,
working and in play, like a song,
that was the song of all-day-long,
which varied life, and all our days,
and verified our life.

BOOK V

(Early Poems, 1963 – 1976)

LEMON LIGHT

ON AN AFTERNOON IN AUGUST

On an afternoon in August
His mind was filled
Like a light room with lilies.

Suddenly the curtains had become
Lithe and spinnakering on the wind,
Graceful as a poem by Ungaretti.

He was pierced by a sense of things
Sharp as the smell of fresh cut lemons,
While the dancers sang to him:

Hèlas mon pauvre gentilhomme,
C'est l'éclat de nos fraîches haleines!

POEM

Which did I love
first, your body or
the pinks and grasses of
the garden? Was it
the shape of leaves
enchanted first
my hands, or
your soft breasts?
or was it the line
and fall of hair
taught me delight
of shadows? Who
taught me first
the grace of nakedness—
exhalations of
the earth, or
maidenfern, or
was it the pinks and
grasses of
your garden?

LEMON LIGHT
For R

As in lemon light a melon brags,
So affluence is found in vines and shadows
And the movement of blue fish.
The affluence of summer is interpreted
In the unintelligible gibber of these leaves.

But for the digressions of pellucid gold
The web might be a cincture of the air;
The heat might be the odor of the earth;
The wind might be the movement of that migratory gray.
So let us call this apogee of green

The resurrection of all splendor,
Innocence piped in the language of small birds,
And peace the projection of full leaves.
Then it happens that your slightest smile
Comes to be a gesture of forgotten grace.

TOILETTE

Out of the window, in the blue air,
The grass is green and the daisies white.
They sway like sailboats, swinging lightly.

Sunlight falls, staining flowers,
Bright light streams on the dressing table.
Red lips and redder nipples,

Your breasts swing lightly as you brush your hair.

FAT TIME

Fat time, the touch of sheets,
The taste of oranges,
Hot water on a tired face;
A glove, a wrist, a hand;

Time flexes like a muscle,
Releases spiritual wings—
A shaft of dappled light,
Voices from a farther room;

The moment at evening
When the upgathered clouds
Release like lightning
Their habitual gold.

WINTER TWILIGHT

Winter twilight like a purer perception,
A new refining at the end of day,
Not an answer but a definition,
And in defining, a precision
Of this to this to this and that to that,
A sudden discovery of the possible.

THE TREE

Green tree in midst of winter, brilliant sign,
Equal in puissance to an angel singing,
No aureate of angel is so fine
As the fine gold that winter will be spinning.

No wealth so wealthy as the wealth you show,
Coeval with the weather, bitter peer;
You wear your crown of laurel and of snow
As a young maiden wears her maiden hair.

And like a maiden trussed up in a tower
You wait upon your hair, spinning your chains,
Singeing the morning with your frosty breath:

"Blasted the bole, the frost is on the flower,
The wind is making powder with its pains.
I sit and sing, outwaiting transient death."

IN DECEMBER

Where I sit the palm trees
Snap in the sun;
I sun with birds and bees,
Oranges and lemon.

I dream, alas, of a land
Tented with snow,
Where forests freeze, and
Midnights pile the silence.

TWO THOUGHTS

i

In the prism of the night,
The geese,
Flying south across the copper of the moon,
Are merely atoms of my thought
Released into a larger loneliness.

ii

I want to tell you something
But I don't know how.
The poem you read flows on like music,
And yet I say that time does not exist.
Even in time
The poem will rest inside you like a thought.

It has happened now.

EXILE

Two windows, two curtains, and the night,
And the sound of crickets:
Their foreign, intermittent burr
Like a ball bearing.

At one window, the garden,
A tale from the Arabian nights;
At the other, the city,
The upturned belly of a fish.

Cars, tires, and the crickets
Like a door in summer,
And the sudden sound of motors
Leapt like Aeolus from his bag—

Who blew Ulysses and his doomèd men
Far from their native shore.
Upon the foreign banks of ocean
They wept with the sound of crickets.

OLD SONG

In the wood there lies a knight
And by his side both day and night

There weeps a maiden and her shroud
Is pied with daisies and with blood

And by that knight there rises a tree
And in the tree black ravens three

Turn to each other and ask their mates
Where shall we our breakfast take?

And one of the heart and one of the head
And one of the liver of the dead

While all around there stretched the wood
And the merry birds sang on.

ALONE

The evening is as delicate and fine
As the perception of death to a child;
It flickers in the corner of the room
Like a moth about a candle.

The shadows are no darker than the rings
Beneath the wonder of the lover's eyes;
Memories, like the small beasts of the forest,
Come to water at her loneliness.

Tender as grass, remonstrant as hours,
The silence is the maker of her powers;
All this will fade, only to be
As one gold ring in the softness of her ear.

AFTER HOFMANNSTAHL
For Tants

As if just yesterday I feel their breath
Wet on my face, the breath of those now gone,
The unapproachable ones wrapped round in death,

The ones familiar as my face or bone.
How can this be, that those remembered years
Are now forever fled, forever gone?

This is a thing that lies too deep for tears,
A frightening thing that no one comprehends:
That all is fleeting, that all disappears,

And that the image which the mirror sends
As intimate as our own face, is just
A gathering from unacknowledged ends,

As private and as common as the dust.

SECRET POEM

In everything there is a god resides,
In the trees and in the stones,
In man's mind and in his very bones—
Unceasingly he waits, and darkling hides.

He is it gives to everything its worth,
Its puissance and its immortality;
His patient fixity
Sustains the pillage of the ancient earth.

His eyes flash fire from the secret stone.
Everywhere I move
I see the passion of his secret love—
Even my secret thoughts, which are his own.

I am the spokesman for his dark despair,
Locked as he is within the chemical;
He is the Titan there
Within the germ, the molecule, the cell.

Like man, he labors on unceasingly,
Through myriad changes trying to express
Archetypal consciousness,
The groan of the creation to be free.

BELIEVE ME, LOVE

Believe me, love, they are not wrong who claim
This world is welded in a single flame,
And waits in patience for us to perceive,
    Though we do not believe.

Nor wrong who tell us that the mind is whence
Stretched this one realizable world of sense,
The only Garden and the only Town,
    Although we all confound.

How would it be, if everything we know
Were nothing but a pantomime, a show?
Where would we be, if all were so consigned,
    But moving round stone blind?

Or say that the mind is impotent to seize
The world in its particularities;
Where could those primal atoms claim to be
    But mired in mystery?

The whole creation harbors this desire,
To be consumed in one perceptual fire,
Not frozen in a geometric form,
    But breathing, live, and warm.

Help me, love, to make this world to be,
Help me to know this one reality,
Not merely of the heart or of the mind,
    But of the whole condign.

LIKE SHADOWS
SBH

Like shadows do we pass across the earth,
Now here, now gone, and no one can tell where,
Into the earth we go, into the air—
The endless travesty of death and birth.

We melt and float away like summer's rack.
Where can we come to rest, Lord, but in you?
Where in this endless pantomime, this show?
For no one knows the word to call us back.

Surely as pain, as unrecallably,
We float out of the mind and pass away.
Nature remembers nothing. And the few

Who loved us, whom we loved, bewilderedly
Repeat our name, not knowing what they say,
Forgetting already. For they are passing too.

BECAUSE SOME WORDS OF MINE

Because some words of mine have soothed you,
Because my thoughts (already thought by others)
Ease some burden of your own, you turn,

Your thigh upon my thigh, bestowing too much faith.
Yet wisdom, my love, resides with the gods,
Our profoundest words are tinged with longing,

Behind them squirms the ulterior motive.
No one escapes the impotence of the body,
The bluntness and ignorance of the mind;

Finally we must settle for the human,
Though what is human ultimately is useless.
Listen to words, but guess their hidden meaning;

Do not remove your leg when I grow silent.

AT EVENING

As at night the birds have nothing to say,
So his unbelief brought desolation.
He had the images of the eye—
The branch the leaf the tangled vine—
And the terrible tangle of the mind.
It was as if his search for something real
Had led him to the desert of the anchorite.

GNOSIS

There is a secret   difficult to tell,
Known to the wise   and to them but slightly:
The eyes that behold you   they are your eyes,
You meet yourself daily   coming and going.

The glass that shatters   the branch that breaks,
The needles of the pine   the petals of the rose,
The wind that whispers   through intricate stops,
The letters that spell   the unspelt word—

Mind is one   indivisible,
The ground of Being   the source of Becoming,
Universal   upholder of Existence,
Form of all forms   End of all Beginning.

IN MEMORIAM

Even when it is gone we can miss it.
The mind sends out its envoys,
Harbingers of our delicate dreams.

Bees fly, leaves turn and turn,
Light dabbles in the branches.
Under the leaves thoughts lodge like dew.

So we can miss it, though it is gone,
And the sky continues on its journey,
Still sheltering leaves in ineffable light.

HOW WE LIVED

IN RAIN

In Manhattan
the rain slicked streets
flip topsy-turvy,

the roofs of buildings
turn upside down
in glass.

I slog
through a wonder of rain
opening the slicked macadam.

The world is a poem.
I am at home
in this middle kingdom

where being
flounders
in actuality

and wonder
is involuntary celebration.
Plato was right,

The mind is tranced
by the minnow flicks
of becoming,

departing
into darkness.
Elsewhere

(and right here)
the hurtful
hateful actual

smudges the page.
I breathe
the complicity I am.

Rain pelts
the macerated cardboard,
candies

the incomprehensible
flotsam and jetsam
of the real—

while under us
the world
turns topsy-turvy

in puddles,
in poetry,
in rain.

MARK IT DOWN

A long time ago we were immortal.
I remember the happiness, like a flavor,
and the colors.
Of course there was no Garden,
only people living together,
squabbles,
the usual things, and occasionally
something bigger;
but no one suspected Failure,
and consequently there was a kind of Innocence,
though mostly, I suppose,
it was a question of other things,
the touch of a hand
the sound of a voice,
the beauty of objects that left you hungry,
as if beauty were a sort of deprivation,
an astonishment without resolution—
it is hard to define,
this Innocence,
and anyway, it was a lie
(though I don't know what is so special
about the truth),
but nonetheless I wanted to mark it down
before we forget,
to mark it down
that once, a long time ago,
we were immortal.

CHILDHOOD

They live in a sharp land.
Sunlight falls,
Slicing shadows. Their voices,
Strident as goslings,
Weave in the playground.
Their games
Resurrect the heroes:
Paris, the pretty boy,
Achilles, and Helen,
Breathless as a skinned knee.
What they know is graspable and tastes like pennies—
Flesh, sweat, earth.
They chase each other with sticks,
Piss against bushes . . . while the afternoon
Slips slowly toward eternity. They
Never suspect they are leaving.
Sometimes they fondle shamelessly.
And when they get angry and throw themselves down,
They don't protect their skulls.

VIOLENCE AND BEAUTY

Spring has flowered and distress
Blossoms into loveliness,
Every woman whom I see
Argues immortality.

Every paper that I read
Argues that the neck must bleed,
Argues that the spring be met
With the gun and bayonet.

May has got into the gland,
Into the thighbone and the hand,
Dogs and sparrows mount and swell,
Busy and impersonal.

Something hard and serpentine
Writhes within the writhing vine,
Swells the flower and the tree
With a yet known savagery.

Violence and beauty meet
In the bloody savage beat
Of the bloody savage heart,
Where the savage got his start.

Something catches blood and soul
Into an unpardoned whole
With a force that yet puts on
All the brilliance of the sun.

1967

A. Whatever formed the autumn formed her thighs.
The wind comes howling with its dripping hands,
Fracturing leaves.
All day in a passion of confusion
The trees stood up on end.

Her body became a point of meaning,
A particle of violence,
Something connected in the politics of misery.
It was as if the ultimate voice
Were a rattle in the larynx.

All day in the ripeness of the air
Her breasts her lips her hair
Became the centers of despair,
As if the mind were the growth of fingernails,
The intimacy of leaves.

B. My friend, what use is that vagina
When we lard the fields of China?

ON A POLITICAL FIGURE

In the quiet and the stillness there
I saw a lovely woman lying down,
One of her tan and shapely breasts was bare,
Her gut was ripped and slipped onto the ground.

The human figure is a form divine—
Or so at least the ancient poets have sung.
And yet the world—that baboon's great behind—
Finds its image soiled in its own dung.

THIS VIOLENCE OF RAGE AND LOVE

This violence of rage and love
Is now become the only flower,
The single stem upon which all is gathered.
Ascend the stair, the broken tower,
The beaten pinnacle of love,
Where blessedness in fiery flower
Blesses the chaos of its power,
The rape the murder and the heat
And violence that must create
The inextinguishable mundane.

The corded fire and the nerve
That twist the passion and the flame
Into the perishable brain,
Bind in one supreme cement
The perishable lineament,
The tension and its curve.

PAIN THAT WON'T DIE

I'm thinking now of where this thing must tend,
There's no denying, something has been shot.
Pain that won't die and grief that will not end.

There's no pretending when one can't pretend,
The past is present, whether we like or not.
I'm thinking now of where this thing must tend,

It's simple things I'll never comprehend.
The difficulty must lie in the gut—
Pain that won't die and grief that will not end.

We plead and argue but the thing won't bend,
The heart's as hard and stubborn as a knot.
I'm thinking now of where this thing must tend,

I don't see how it's ever going to mend;
It comes again even when we've forgot,
Pain that won't die and grief that will not end.

You close your eyes and speak as to a friend.
God knows the cure for what we two have got!
I'm thinking now of where this thing must tend:

Pain that won't die and grief that will not end.

BAJAZETH

The poet starts out on his virgin page
Erecting gardens for the mind of man
Wherein he hopes to find a Golden Age,
Utopia, and Fields Elysian.
He ends, however, mindless in his rage,
Like Bajazeth abloodied in his cage.

DEATH IN PARIS

i

After his coronary
My father thrashed and kicked
And wouldn't stay in bed.

They had to drug him
So that anger wouldn't kill him.
Meanwhile in Paris

The chestnuts died stately,
And the people on the boulevards
Whooped and farted

As if there had never been two wars.
That night we made love in the bathtub,
Your breasts bobbing like pink seals.

At midnight we sent a telegram:
Dear Dad,
Love love love.

In the middle of the night I woke
Sweating my sheets,
Like a child who pisses on his mattress.

ii

I cannot understand this grief
That chokes me like a bone.

Something ruptures in my chest that is not me
And yet is only me.

Gagged and hounded by love,
I cry out in a voice gone silent with longing,
In a language I feared to have forgotten,
Like a prophet visited by tongues.

                iii
I can come to no terms with this thing
That kicks me in the teeth.

Imagination reels like a subway
Or stays stable,

It makes no difference,
Nothing brings comprehension.

Dearer than chocolate,
Unthinkable as distance,

You have ceased to be wordable,
Like a dream,

And in dreams alone I find you,
Familiar as light,

Common as bread or language,
And utterly gone.

O strange strange strange!

I have learned I am nothing and have forgotten,

Like a demonstration in geometry.
Strictly speaking, with the philosophers,

All is absurdity,
Mere disappearing.

Pain remains, but not you,
Who were sweet and difficult as poetry.

iv

For five weeks
My father lay dying,
Coughing and hacking
While somewhere
In a different country
I walked and talked.

Somewhere there is a man
With hair darker than mine,
With chest and arms and belly
Larger than mine,
Somewhere, lost forever.

I think of Emerson,
Who taught that mind is universal,
Learning, in frigid wisdom,
That he had forgotten his son;
Of Proust,

Who wanted love,
And proved in his bedroom
That love is passing,
Writing in solitude
That all must be lost.

And yet both claimed
That nothing is forgotten,
Stored, every particle,
In secret memory,
To stop us suddenly
With terrible justice.

Wherever I turn you hurt me,
So that everywhere
A giant stands in my way.
Trapped like love within the body,
Where could I reach
That you would not extend?

IN HEGEL'S PHENOMENOLOGY OF MIND

In Hegel's *Phenomenology of Mind*
Objects are defined by the negative.

Light describes the black holes of the universe,
I am not what surrounds me,

You are not.
Your absence is defined by the world,

The world by your absence.
A Nothing haunts us

Dearer than color
In the swift precipitations of autumn.

When I awake
Your absence is a presence more real

Than walls. Discrepancies
Of consciousness shake up

The actual. I see
Toward the limiting case,

Which is zero, and there alone
I find you. It is dear—

It costs too much. And yet
Across the hard wood floor

Nothingness shakes like the light.

It is probably a lie that you existed

It is probably a lie that you existed.

It is probably a lie that a year ago, beneath leaves,
We stopped by the side of a road
And looked from the top of a hill.
It is probably a lie that your hands,
Veined and handsome,
Held things in a certain manner,
Or that your singing sounded in the morning.

But since it is a lie, it is probably a lie
That I existed, since there I am beside you,
Holding your hand and looking up a bit quizzically.
It is probably a lie that either of us existed,
Or is a dream we shared together,
A dream we shared in the early hours of the morning
When the walls go white with sunlight.

It is probably a lie that *existence* existed,
Or is more than a dream we shared together,
Since you never existed . . . or I never existed . . .
Or we never existed together . . .
Or we still exist together, somewhere lost together . . .

(Though there is water still in the palm of my hand
That has passed from your palm forever).

PYRAMID

Now in my mind I can see
The generations come trooping
Into the valley of the living,
The generations of the departed.

I see them in my mind
Like gentle waves of sleep,
Fold after fold together
Gathered as round a flower.

In rank they come and in file
Trooping slowly together
To behold the newly begotten
The newest of the living.

And they bend in benediction
And smile in approval,
Beholders utterly forgotten
Beholders never to be forgotten.

For this small life for the moment
Is the apex of the pyramid,
The generations of the living,
The generations of the departed.

IN MEMORIAM

For fifty-seven years you peered
From out our insular emptiness
Onto a world not worth your anxiety.

Now emptiness has called to emptiness.
Yet standing before this place or fact,
I wonder how you would have thought or acted.

Peculiar and beloved, may your kind heart
Rest quiet in the haven of the just,
Though it be only in the homage of the passing.

VARIATION ON A THEME BY WILBUR

Even when love began
Our eager glands to swell,
And moved our eager hearts
Brimful with love's blood,
There was another place
I saw with a sudden start,
Saw for an instant's spell
Behind the tight skullpan,
There where the creature stood
Impenitent as ice.

Even when we had known
Love ripened to completion,
Had savored to the full
The golden grain and plumbed
Into the golden gourd,
There was another tone
Of light on street or hill,
Another cruel secretion,
A cruel, indifferent word
To which the heart succumbed.

Even when we could say
Love had bestowed its gift
Of daring discipline,
Its proper liberty,
Something else would still
Stalk the glittering day,

Or into the night would drift
With its appalling will
Of truant licensee,
Even though we would win.

DEATH AND THE WEATHER

He awoke to a fear new and familiar
As the odor of burnt leaves.
Something was dying,

He caught it in the ozone of the air.
The first full flush of etiolation
Burnished the clouds like pennies.

It was a dyeing within the crystal hemisphere,
A McIntoshing to a coral russet
Familiar as any fluttering.

Oxidation brilloed the trees.
It manumitted beauty like
A nude descending the stairs.

His head spun round
As if he sensed the shift of the axis,
The sleight of vertigo that brought in

Death and the weather.
Something was suffocating, he knew it in
The wind, vilipend,

Roughing the mild appendages.
The intercalation of shadows
Coalesced to ideology.

The whole contraption had come down
With death, like the flu,
And no one would escape.

THE DAY THE TREES STOPPED EXISTING

On the day the trees stopped existing
There was no thunder.
It wasn't that the trees appeared different;
There weren't any. It was like a metaphysician
Forgetting his arguments.
Dogs sniffed at the hydrants,
Clouds appeared in the windows of cars.
It was a major concession to stupidity.

OCTOBER EXERCISE

i

What is given remains
the spectacular.
One might mention
the one maple
scarlet at the edges.
In a perfect blue
quirky birds
punctuate the sky.

ii

I saw New England gray
above the shabby town of Cambridge
announcing nothing good,

while seaward beating
the long winged gulls of the Atlantic
beat onward toward the sea.

iii

I heard the trees singing
while from the east
sun lacquered the
ramshackled regalia
of the tenements.

iv

This exemplary show
of sunshine is

exemplary but
brash and cocky
the sparrows are
cocky and hopeless
as a poem by Williams.

v
between
words and shadows
my daughter
discovers the world.

vi
Dancing!
my daughter
dancing
cries
as

leaflike
she twirls on
the twirling carpet
like a leaf-
twirled
shadow.

vii
On Massachusetts Avenue
I met who
accompanied me for

several blocks that
carefree dog who
all day hums love
O careless love.

    viii
The pomp of this levée
is somewhat punctured
by the muskrat footmat
by the door stoop.

    ix
The odor of fresh coffee is
not less delightful than
sunlight or Couperin
on the cranky radio.

    x
It only took
one crossing on
the Red Line
to appreciate the
sail studded waters of
the Charles.

    xi
We hung
the stained glass high
above
the slatternly dumps
of Cambridge.

Watch out it doesn't fall!

xii
You lucky son-of-a-bitch,
he yelled,
being ten years old,
and I thought

you lucky son-of-a-bitch
raised
in the United States
of America.

xiii
It was apparent from the light
that even the window was
under water.

xiv
Like floaters on the retina
the birds moved at the edge of the visible
into nothing.

xv
Above the week's accumulation of garbage
the blue bottle flies
are only shadows to
the quick electric politics of
the yellow jackets.

xvi

O indefeasible ball!
with all my might I
hurl you into the water,

where
for a while you disappear to
remerge, pop!

on the surface
bob bob bob.
(So with you,

my father,
who come back out of dreams
to greet me.)

xvii

Intelligence is an unfriendly friend.

Spit the pit out of the mouth,
and spit out the mealy apple.

xviii

If one were seeking aid
(and one is)
the sun blanch on the bay
might dispirit,
whose coruscations
pall comparison.

xix

Ten years ago I
first heard
the recital of
the leaves

playing the partita
in C minor.

xx

Is it the fracture in the mind enjoys
the undulant weird beauty of
the fractured window?

xxi

Even the sun this bright October day
might black
were it professor of another word than gold.

xxii

Eidolon you say
while beyond the window
autumn wags its thousand tongued
paraphernalia

xxiii

In the gray glass window
an airplane
cutting the sky!

xxiv

It wasn't so much the leaves
as the one leaf that skipped across the road

nor even that
as the sharp tang of the air

nor even that
as the rough wind

brandishing its scimitar, that
confounded the philosophers.

xxv

Sharpen your knives,
poet!

the world awaits
carving.

xxvi

The leaves
jerk and twist
on the branch
like
so many
hanged men.

xxvii

Not one leaf has ever been expressed.
No, nor ever will.

xxviii

Although success be ninety percent renunciation,
he lifted anchor and beat downwind,
awaiting instruction.

xxix

"The endless à priori of the mind,
taking in the world,"
which is of course
its à priori.

xxx

Behold!
this stone this leaf this valley.

xxxi

As you pass
the new
construction,
do not neglect
the fresh odor
of the raw-
cut pine.

xxxii

Should you trip,
you would fall   forward

into being.

xxxiii
In my poverty
I was daily sub-
sidized by
my friends
the trees.

xxxiv
One by one
and then in handfuls
rain
strips the leaves.
Soon
none will be left
for the teeth
of winter.
What can we say
before
this spectacle
this tragedy?

We live
in a beautiful world.

xxxv
Wag wag wag wag wag
dangle dangle
flip flop flutter
saffron
        yellow
                turn

yellowsaffron
        shimmer
shake shake shake
shudder dangle down

     drop

    xxxvi
In the essential spaces of the sky
the inessential leaves
swerve and blow like the atoms of Lucretius.

    xxxvii
These are the poems of an American,
that fit, dustlike,
into corners.

    xxxviii
In the poverty of
early winter
only the willow
trails its gold
to celebrate

the birth of tragedy.

THE THINGS THAT MAKE US CRY
For Helen Armstrong

You ascend the stairs,
kids clasping like barnacles,

a wisp of hair
caught to a perspiring forehead—

a woman I hardly know
(dear acquaintance, dear friend!)

to whom I've never talked
sex or politics,

a firehat offered diffidently for
my girl:

"we won't stay but a minute,
I don't want to cry."

Lovely woman!
consider mortality,

your father doddering, or mine
so distant

I meet him almost safely
in dreams—

these things
the things that make us cry,

a parting on the stairs forever
of mere acquaintances.

THE LEAVES ARE BLOWN UPWARD

Upward in the autumn air
The leaves like confetti are blown,
Turning and turning.

Into the sky they go, into the blue,
The flicks and phonemes of sight,
The pure hussahs: "evanid,

Whiffling, and fantastic things,"
The saltimbanques, the rootless.
Mounting they go, twirling,

Poor restless flicks,
Blasted and blustered and blown,
Until they lose their way,

Like any mortal thing,
And flutter back to earth,
The appointed,

To moulder down.

SMALL POEMS FOR R

i

Chestnuts sizzle on the brazier,
Flare a moment, then a moment.
Wind whips the schoolgirls' kilts.

Light crashes against a window,
A taxi grinds and swerves,
A gray squirrel zig-zags for a corner.

This is you, love, this is you,
Autumn up and down the avenue,
Love so deep we hardly know it's there . . .

The shell splits open in the acrid air.

ii

Sun spits in sequence
on cellophane,
aluminum foil,
mica in the pavement.

An ambulance
sparks the avenue.
A tree flares—
one finger in the eye of god.

iii

Steam shovels
maw the chewed-up pavement,

their Saurian mouths
drip vegetable. Man builds,
the yak-yak of his chain saw
rips the air.
                   Leaves
lick up dirt,
changing carbon monoxide
into oxygen.
Bulldozers maneuver the potholes.

I stand in the park,
eyeing the park.
Love didn't build this city, love.
Man did.

                   iv
The winch chains grind and haul—
a bucket of blood.

Smoke
monkeywrenches in the sky.

The pipes knock-knock,
and coke liquefies at 1000 degrees.

The scrag heap of the heart
burns in the washed out gully.

                   v
The subway shunts and pounds,
a megaton jackhammer.

Electricity courses the line. Love,
I still remember one rhyme:

The fat rat dodges the third-rail's lip.
The entire rattle-trap subway smells of shit.

vi

Love, the root has tackled the wire,
They grip like rigor mortis . . . .

Hard things count, the face
Lashed by a thousand thoughts,

The old man with arthritic knuckles.
I'll love you when the nail has turned to rust.

Love lies crucified in the chemical.

vii

This snow that melts
before it touches
(hypertrophied crystals of water

fluffing to beauty:
the down of the chick
wide-eyed in terror) . . .

I remember snow
circling the branches—
an echo

receding to nothing.

       viii
I saw the trees
incarnadined
against the sky,
the grasses
hop
to the wind's splutter,
the nettles
stuck
in the tongue

in endless passion.

DULL LEAVES IN GRAMERCY PARK

The leaves are dead.
What once was color

Is a palpable absence,
Hazy as bronze,

A kind of meditation
In a sleepy cranium.

Not the hectic exuberance
Of October, the heterodox—

The cry of an animal
Pulsing like genius,

But a crematorial monochrome
Smokey as evening,

The quiet of middle age
Headed toward a stillness

Deep and persistent as ignorance
And as certain.

SNOW

Nothing could be more
Flurry-white-beautiful as
Shaken free floating
Caught-on-a-current upward
It eddied and crossed the curve
Of sight
To cover the earth.

And I said,
It covers the earth,
And saw that instant
The earth, and recalled
The crusting of garbage with
Bloomed-as-on-power lines
Snow,

And said,
It covers the dead,
And savored that second
The hutched and huddled
The tenement living,
And savvied
Its secret,
It fell
With burst-as-from-cotton pod whiteness

And covered the earth.

THE WAY IT IS

Winter, with its radical mastectomy.
A heatless sun
Oozes like a burst sack
And can't erect a shadow.
Things get lopped, get cropped,
Get cut down to size.

Beneath the sky
The city is an old woman
Poking for empty bottles. Somewhere
A man is tossed from a truck. Somewhere
Bodies are piled by a wall. Somewhere
A child is tied to a radiator.

People make love in every position,
In every combination;
Feet flop like dung in the snow.
A blackness the color of bile
Blots up the sky . . . And yet—

Being is ecstasy! The coin of flesh
Torn by the frozen handle.
Light points on broken bottles along the tops of walls,
Shadows loom at the center,
Along the edges of existence,
The sun glitters on icicles that won't melt.

CELEBRATION!

All day the snow fattened into rain,
White churning to a sluttish gray.
The heart splutters like a motor that won't catch.

The eye feeds on this liquid sacrament,
This sooty sickly seagreen seasick slobber,
This flotsam and jetsam masticated to mush.

Celebration! A glaucous sheen puddles the park,
Scum on the dirt brown of the weeds.
What hides beneath these filthy bandages?

This excremental epiphany of trash?
A transom of sunlight pierces the avenue,
The fin of the Island sharpens like a thought,

The lungs intoxicate in the intolerable air!

SIMPLE THINGS

This year you should have turned sixty,
You were stopped as a younger man.
But since to me we can never be parted,
Look, I see you turn!
Look, I see you stand and smile!

Dear father lost in time,
How I should love to tell you simple things!
Spring is come, the dogwoods
Burst in inexplicable, familiar flame.
Sometimes I ache all night with missing you.

HOW WE LIVE

Now the leaves loll out their tongues
Like lazy animals. Summer!
Another generation of sticky green.
Light shimmers on the face of buildings,
Glints on the city's glitter and glop.

The lust of the eye connects us to the world,
The women in their too tight designer jeans.
The clouds are strung out like lingerie.
We cram life with both hands,
Reveling in the particular!

It is the universal by which man lives.
In the flux and jelly
Form is born in the miracle of becoming.
How to live? What to do?
The contradiction in the belly,
The dialectic in the blood and bone,

The sudden illumination at the top of the stairs.

I LIVE IN TERROR

I live in terror of arriving there,
Crossing the frontier into alien air,
Without my passport, with my passport bare;

So that behind me like a dried honeycomb
The labyrinthine region of our home
Stretches away, a barren decatome,

Where instantly the mountain and the rose
Are stilled together in a like repose,
And nothing comes, and nothing ever goes,

But all lies frozen: tower, sea, and town
Lie lapsed together in a single frown
Of light and shadow where the light pours down.

And Nothing beats about them, and its flame
Licks at the light and shadow with the same
Remorseless silence on that silent plain.

And coming to the keeper of that place
A dread will seize me that his common face
Reflects the visage of my own disgrace,

And that behind me where the common city
Burns on the human plain, the home of pity
Was left behind me irrevocably,

And now we bear the burden of our shame:
Our own accreted share of praise or blame
Is scrivened now as our eternal name.

O save me from this terror and this dread,
Nights of long labor for the living bread,
And claim me for the living from the dead.

CODA:
ACCOUNTING, 2012

For the hundredth,
for the ten hundredth time,
you mount the stairs,
you listen to the sacred singing ....

We stand in brightest light
in deepest shadow. Follow
the twirling spindle,
fill the vase with lilacs.

Wisdom sucks up moisture like a flower.

An hour, a second, and
voices spoken in anger,
discord in a family, consciousness
hacked with an axe.

Now
the moment is flashing
headlong in a sharksong
of eating, in the frenzy
of bloodlust and spring.

Mist fills up the valley ...
your daughter is herself
mist out of the valley,
the merest mist ...

Death comes like justice.

But the dance continues—
as when the women pause,
but the music keeps playing:

they sway into the music,
into the circle of the music,
for there will always be music,
there will always be young women,
there will always be black waves

crashing on a distant shore.

POSTSCRIPT

The preceding collection represents forty years of writing poetry. To see the poems collected in this manner inspires feelings of satisfaction and bemusement. I remember writing most of the poems, some of them when I was an adolescent.

Each poem tries to catch a significant event: a particular emotion—or a thought-as-emotion—in a particular time and place; and attempts to marshal the words, images, music, that will embody that emotion or thought so as to convey it to the reader. How successful I have been I am of course not qualified to say.

As a young man I thought, If only I can write a hundred poems! The number at least has long since been surpassed. I am thankful to the muse. JJH

ACKNOWLEDGMENTS

Various of these poems have appeared previously in *Epos, The RTL Proxy, Inkwell, Best Poems of 1976,* and a chapbook published by Sol Invictus Press. The author has lost track of other such publications, but he offers credit and thanks to all.

He also wishes to offers thanks to his mother and father, his brother Peter, and his two daughters, as well as to the late Henry Wells, Alice Quinn, Karen Steinmetz, Karen Sirabian, Joanna and Bill Herman, and Sr. Ruth Dowd, for their encouragement. Special tribute is paid to Ronnie, the author's beloved wife and companion of 60 years, and to Naomi Rosenblatt, the editor and publisher of this volume.

FOR NAOMI ROSENBLATT

A rose is a rose,
But the leaf of the rose
Helps the rose so
The red rose can grow;
Refreshes the air
So the rose can repair,
By breathing, its red
From dull gray instead;
So all can agree
That rose poetry
Comes from the leaf
That aids us to breathe—
Just like the red rose
And the leaf of the rose.

John Herman grew up in the outskirts of New York City. He received a Doctorate in English Literature from the University of California at Berkeley, and has taught at the Sorbonne (*Paris IV*), and the University of Massachusetts in Boston. He then worked in Manhattan as an editor, first at Simon and Schuster, then as the Editorial Director of Weidenfeld & Nicolson, and then of Ticknor & Fields, a division of Houghton Mifflin. For fifteen years he was the Associate Director of the Graduate Writing Program at Manhattanville College.

Besides poems, essays, two picture books, and a chapbook of poetry, Herman has published four novels, *The Weight of Love* (selected by *Publishers Weekly* as one of the best novels of the year), and *The Light of Common Day* (both Nan Talese Books), as well as *Deep Waters* and *Labyrinth* (both Philomel Books). Mr. Herman resides with his wife in New York City and Canaan, New York. They have two daughters and six grandchildren.

CPSIA information can be obtained
at www.ICGtesting.com
Printed in the USA
BVHW030703231021
619695BV00004B/37